THE EVERYTHING

LARGE-PRINT TRAVEL WORD SEARCH BOOK

VOLUME II

Dear Reader,

Life is a journey. You better bring some puzzles! Wherever you go, these word search puzzles are here for you. They're a nice way to fill an extra moment or two—perhaps on a trip to an exotic locale, or just taking a break at home.

I designed these puzzles for people who love to go places. Each puzzle has a theme that is somehow related to travel: where we go, how we get there, and what we do when we arrive. We printed this book using large letters to make solving the puzzles more pleasant. No eyestrain is required!

So don't forget this book the next time you pack. It's the perfect travel companion. And when you're not traveling, perhaps these puzzles will bring back happy memories of past adventures or dreams of future excursions. I hope you have an enjoyable time on your journey through these pages and wherever your travels take you.

Charles Timmerman

Welcome to the EVERYTHING® Series!

These handy, accessible books give you all you need to tackle a difficult project, gain a new hobby, comprehend a fascinating topic, prepare for an exam, or even brush up on something you learned back in school but have since forgotten.

You can choose to read an Everything® book from cover to cover or just pick out the information you want from our four useful boxes: e-questions, e-facts, e-alerts, and e-ssentials. We give you everything you need to know on the subject, but throw in a lot of fun stuff along the way, too.

We now have more than 400 Everything® books in print, spanning such wide-ranging categories as weddings, pregnancy, cooking, music instruction, foreign language, crafts, pets, New Age, and so much more. When you're done reading them all, you can finally say you know Everything®!

PUBLISHER Karen Cooper
MANAGING EDITOR, EVERYTHING® SERIES Lisa Laing
COPY CHIEF Casey Ebert
ASSOCIATE PRODUCTION EDITOR Mary Beth Dolan
ACQUISITIONS EDITOR Lisa Laing
EVERYTHING® SERIES COVER DESIGNER Erin Alexander

Visit the entire Everything® series at *www.everything.com*

THE EVERYTHING

LARGE-PRINT

TRAVEL

WORD SEARCH

BOOK

VOLUME II

Circle the world with easy-to-read
word search puzzles

Charles Timmerman
Founder of Funster.com

Adams Media
New York London Toronto Sydney New Delhi

Adams Media
An Imprint of Simon & Schuster, Inc.
100 Technology Center Drive
Stoughton, MA 02072

An Everything® Series Book.
Everything® and everything.com® are registered trademarks of Simon & Schuster, Inc.

ADAMS MEDIA and colophon are trademarks of Simon and Schuster.

For information about special discounts for bulk purchases, please contact Simon & Schuster Special Sales at 1-866-506-1949 or business@simonandschuster.com.

The Simon & Schuster Speakers Bureau can bring authors to your live event. For more information or to book an event contact the Simon & Schuster Speakers Bureau at 1-866-248-3049 or visit our website at www.simonspeakers.com.

Manufactured in the United States of America

16 2023

Library of Congress Cataloging-in-Publication Data has been applied for.

ISBN 978-1-4405-6682-0

Dedicated to my family.

Acknowledgments

I would like to thank each and every one of the more than half a million people who have visited my website, *www.funster.com*, to play word games and puzzles. You have shown me how much fun puzzles can be and how addictive they can become!

It is a pleasure to acknowledge the folks at Adams Media who made this book possible. I particularly want to thank my editor, Lisa Laing, for so skillfully managing the many projects we have worked on together.

Contents

Introduction

The puzzles in this book are in the traditional word search format. Words in the list are hidden in the puzzle in any direction: up, down, forward, backward, or diagonal. The words are always found in a straight line, and letters are never skipped. Words can overlap. For example, the two letters at the end of the word "MAST" could be used as the start of the word "STERN." Only uppercased letters are used, and any spaces in an entry are removed. For example, "TROPICAL FISH" would be found in the puzzle as "TROPICALFISH." Apostrophes and hyphens are also omitted in the puzzles. Draw a circle around each word that you find. Then cross the word off the list so that you will always know which words remain to be found.

A favorite strategy is to look for the first letter in a word, then see if the second letter is in any of the neighboring letters, and so on until the word is found. Or instead of searching for the first letter in a word, it is sometimes easier to look for letters that stand out, like *Q*, *U*, *X*, and *Z*. Double letters in a word will also stand out and be easier to find. Another strategy is to simply scan each row, column, and diagonal looking for any words.

Puzzles

ALBANIA

ANDORRA

ART

ATLANTIC OCEAN

AUSTRIA

BALTIC SHIELD

BELGIUM

BLACK SEA

CONTINENT

CULTURAL

ESTONIA

FINLAND

FRANCE

GREECE

GULF STREAM

ICELAND

IRON CURTAIN

LATVIA

LIECHTENSTEIN

LITHUANIA

LUXEMBOURG

MALTA

MONACO

MONTENEGRO

ROME

SLOVAKIA

SLOVENIA

SPAIN

SWEDEN

SWITZERLAND

UKRAINE

VATICAN CITY

```
I C E L A N D L E C N A R F
C A S P A I N A U H T I L Q
A R O U O L A R N M A L T A
A I T D K R I L U I U E M O R
K N L R G E R T A I K Y G R
A E E A E C E L T G G T R O
V N I I N H Z U R L U I U D
O I H N E T T C U E L C O N
L T S E T E I E C B F N B A
S N C V N N W C N L S A M U
S O I O O S S E O A T C E S
W C T L M T W E R C R I X T
E A L S J E R R I K E T U R
D N A L N I F G M S A A L I
E O B A I N O T S E M V N A
N M J A I N A B L A T V I A
```

Solution on Page 300

CABANA	LOCKERS
CEMENT	LOUNGE
CHAIR	OUTDOOR
CHLORINE	PLAY
CLEAN	RETREAT
CROWDED	ROBE
DEEP	RULES
FAMILY	SAFE
GATE	SAUNA
GUESTS	SHALLOW
GUNITE	SHOWERS
HEATED	SNACKS
HOT TUB	SOAK
HOURS	SPA
INDOOR	SWIM
INFINITY	TILE
JACUZZI	TOWEL
JETS	UMBRELLA
KIDS	
LAGOON	
LAPS	
LEISURE	

```
J E T S K C F Q C H Z W R I
S O T S H E A T E D S O E K
E D M A Q N M H O X O L T A
F H I C G A I A O D X L R V
A R W K H E L D T U W A E I
S Q S I D L Y U I C R H A B
Z P S S E C O A N A T S T K
I C A R D R P R F B T H Q N
Z E B L W S U R I A O O R A
Z M U K O K C S N N W W S U
U E T E R C V P I A E E O D
C N T R C A K E T E L R A E
A T O I N N J E Y U L S K L
J B H U N S X D R O O D N I
E Y A L P U G U E S T S C T
A S D N O O G A L O U N G E
```

Solution on Page 300

ANIMALS

ANTIQUITIES

BONES

BRONZE

CERAMICS

CLOTHING

DINOSAURS

DIORAMA

DISCOVERIES

DOCUMENTS

DRAWINGS

EXAMPLES

FINE ART

FOSSIL

FURNITURE

GLASS

GUARDS

GUIDE

HALLS

METALWORK

MODEL

MOVIES

MUMMY

MYSTERIES

PAINTING

PORTRAIT

ROPES

SCULPTURE

SKELETON

SPECIMENS

STONE

TOOLS

TOUR

WEAPONRY

```
M U M M Y R N O P A E W Q X
N A C C B D I O R A M A G M
O E N S G N I W A R D N U Y
T Z U T P A I N T I N G I S
E N S E I R E V O C S I D T
L O C H U Q F O S S I L E E
E R U T P L U C S T A G R R
K B H A L L S I R S L U K I
S L A M I N A A T A V A R E
S P E C I M E N S I X R O S
E M S T O N E S D X E D W E
N O S C I M A R E C P S L I
O D R F U R N I T U R E A V
B E U C L O T H I N G M T O
S L O O T S E L P M A X E M
P D T I A R T R O P E S M K
```

AGRICULTURE

ALEXANDER CITY

AUBURN

AUTAUGA COUNTY

CAMELLIA

CONECUH

COOSA RIVER

DAUPHIN ISLAND

DOTHAN

FLORENCE

FORT MITCHELL

GADSDEN

HALEYVILLE

HEART OF DIXIE

LONGLEAF PINE

MADISON

MOUNT CHEAHA

PHENIX CITY

PLANTATION

SAND ISLAND

SELMA

SOUTHEASTERN

TALLADEGA

THORNHILL

WETUMPKA

```
E N I P F A E L G N O L Y C
C A T H O R N H I L L T P A
O G F L O R E N C E I D Z M
O E C O N E C U H C Z N X E
S D O T H A N C R L C A H L
A A K P M U T E W O R L E L
R L N O S I D A M L E S A I
I L I L M N R U B U A I R A
V A U T A U G A C O U N T Y
E T R X P L A N T A T I O N
R O E L L I V Y E L A H F E
F L Y T I C X I N E H P D D
A G R I C U L T U R E U I S
F M O U N T C H E A H A X D
X O S A N D I S L A N D I A
N R E T S A E H T U O S E G
```

Solution on Page 300

ACREAGE

ANIMALS

BARN

BLISSFUL

BROOK

BUGS

CAT

CHICKENS

CORN

COWS

CROPS

DAIRY

DIRT

DOG

FAMILY

FARM

FENCE

FIELDS

GARDEN

GRAIN

HARVEST

HORSES

LEMONADE

NATURE

OVERALLS

PASTURE

PIGS

PORCH

POULTRY

RANCH

RODEO

RURAL

SHEEP

SIMPLE

SLOWER

SNAKES

TOWN

TRACTOR

TREES

WHEAT

```
K T T A E H W O M P S M D W
X O D N C S E C O W S I B G
X V O N V D N R O C R B S U
X E A R O T C A R T Y N G S
C R V R B H S F K L P Y I B
J A C R E A G E I E P R P U
B L T X T D M M V E S I E G
A L E M O N A D E R L A E S
R S I G W F P A A U A D H L
N B E S N A Y Z N M L H S O
I N U S S N E K C I H C I W
T E A T R F L M S I M P L E
R D U T P O U L T R Y A C R
E R J R U I H L A O R N L B
E A S P O R C F W U E F U S
S G R A I N E Y R F N O G G
```

Solution on Page 301

ACADIA

ACURA MDX

CARGO

COMPACT SUV

DIRT ROADS

DODGE JOURNEY

DURANGO

ENCORE

EXPEDITION

GRAND CHEROKEE

HUMVEE

JEEP COMPASS

KIA SORENTO

LEXUS LX

LIGHT TRUCKS

LUXURY SUV

NISSAN ARMADA

NISSAN MURANO

OIL PRICES

SEATS

STATION WAGON

TAHOE

TOYOTA SEQUOIA

TRAILBLAZER

WRANGLER

YUKON

```
K X U U O I L P R I C E S E
I W R A N G L E R K X K O R
S S D A O R T R I D C N N O
T O Y O T A S E Q U O I A C
A T S R E N U H R I S D R N
T N E E I D A T T S O I U E
I E A B O C T I A D G X M C
O R T O A H D N G K N D N O
N O S D G E A E T H A M A M
W S I I P R J T U D R A S P
A A L X M O A M B O U R S A
G I E A U K V C Y Q D U I C
O K D R L E X U S L X C N T
N A N J E E P C O M P A S S
R E Z A L B L I A R T F F U
Y U K O N L U X U R Y S U V
```

Solution on Page 301

BLACK

BOOK

BRUSH

BUCKLE

CAMERA

CARRY

CHECK

CLAIM

COAT

COMB

DIVIDER

DRESS

FILL

FOLD

GLASSES

HAT

HEAVY

JACKET

LOCK

LOST

MAPS

PACK

PADDED

PANTS

POCKET

POUCH

SHIRTS

SHOES

SIZE

SOAP

SOCKS

STRAP

TAG

TOTE

TOWELS

TRAVEL

TRIP

VALISE

WHEELS

ZIPPER

Suitcase

```
Q A S B C E G B R T E B D J
N F K O X H P A R T S M C P
N T C C A B T M T L C O I A
H R O H S P A M E R H C L O
M A L Y I H R W H E E L S E
T V T R K O O B P P C A I B
T E T C H T R E Q P K I Z X
G L A S S E S Z S I U M E H
X P U H D K L F H Z P S T E
Y R O I H C F K O W I O O A
B Z V R C O I E C L W C T V
D I W T U P L B A U D K S Y
D I J S O Y L V M R B S R B
I D A A P A D D E D W R U L
C Z Y Q C A L S R P A N T S
E O Q K T S S J A C K E T Z
```

Solution on Page 301

ADVANCE

AGENT

ARRIVAL

BALCONY

BED

BOOK

CABIN

CALL

CELEBRATION

COMMITMENT

DATE

DINING

FACILITIES

FLIGHT

GATHERING

GROUP

GUESTS

HOTEL

LIST

NAME

NIGHTS

NOTICE

OCCUPANTS

PAYMENT

PLAN

POOL

RESERVED

RESTAURANT

ROOM

SCHEDULE

SEATING

SITE

SPA

SUITE

TABLE

TICKETS

TIME

TRAIN

VENUE

VILLA

```
N I A R T H P L A N K A P U
S I A B O A G E N T O O U B
P T B T S T N A P U C C O H
A T E A R R I V A L L T R B
C L N K C D R D I N I N G T
S E L A C D E V R E S E R I
C E L I R I H B O G T M U M
H A I E V U T S W N S Y E E
E R L T B D A T E I E A P C
D Y O L I R G T T T U P O O
U N P O E L A E S A G S O O
L O C O M M I T M E N T L P
E C N A V D A C I S R H F T
F L I G H T D N A O E G W L
T A B L E U N E V F N I Z O
W B S U I T E C I T O N Y T
```

Solution on Page 301

ADVENTURE

ARRIVAL

BRIDE

CHERISHED

CHOCOLATE

COUPLE

CRUISE

DINNER

FLIGHT

FUN

GROOM

HAPPY

HARMONY

HUSBAND

ISLAND

JOY

LAUGHTER

LOVE

LUXURY

MARRIAGE

PARADISE

POOL

PRIVATE

QUIET

RELAXING

RESORT

ROMANTIC

ROSES

SECLUDED

SOLITUDE

SPA

SUITE

TRAVEL

TREK

TRIP

TROPICAL

VACATION

VOYAGE

WEDDING

WIFE

28

```
J Q W S U I T E F I W E Y E
O U K E S I U R C O U P L E
Y I P O D S G T R I P L A D
R E N N I D G E G A Y O V I
U T C H E R I S H E D V I R
X D N H O L H N R Z T E R B
U C E O O L A U G H T E R R
L I M D O C T C G Y G Y A X
E G S O U N O I I A T N V T
V N P L E L L L I P R O A R
A I A V A F C R A F O M C E
R X D F U N R E V T S R A K
T A P A R A D I S E E A T C
R L R O M A N T I C R H I X
K E D U T I L O S S E S O R
P R I V A T E H U S B A N D
```

Solution on Page 302

ACCIDENT

ASPHALT

BRAKES

BRIDGES

CAR

CHAINS

COAST

CONTROL

CRASH

CURVES

DRIVER

FOG

FROSTY

FROZEN

GREASE

ICE

INJURIES

LANES

MIST

OIL

PERILOUS

PLOWS

PUDDLES

RAIN

RISKY

SALT

SAND

SKID

SLEET

SLIP

SLOW

SLUSH

SNOW

SPEED

TIRES

TRUCK

UNSAFE

WARNING

WATER

WET

```
Z I T L A S N O W Q W U Q K
W D N A S E V R U C C E C I
W X P P P Z J L I O I U O J
O B I E H M G N I N R A W S
L L O R A C B F J T T F O G
S O Y I L H O U B R R S O E
D H H L T A R A C O E Y I W
S I S O N I A R S L V T D M
L O K U E N E T D T I F E J
U Y K S D S Y D W R R Z E I
S R Q E I H U V E O D G P A
H I C G C P U S Z W R M S P
J S J D C W Q E S E N A L F
H K A I A G N W A T E R E U
U Y B R A K E S W O L P E A
L B A B C L E F A S N U T T
```

Solution on Page 302

ARRIVAL	PUBLIC
BENCH	ROUTE
BLANKET	SCHOOL
BUMPY	SEAT
CHANGE	SENIOR
CHARTER	SIGNAL
CITY	STATION
COACH	STOP
COMMUTE	STUDENT
COST	TICKET
CROWDED	TIMES
DRIVER	TOUR
EXIT	TRANSIT
EXPRESS	TRAVEL
FARE	TRIP
HANDLE	TROLLEY
LOCAL	WAIT
LUGGAGE	WORK
MAP	
PASS	
PILLOW	
PRIVATE	

```
B Z P Y A B P V R P Y C X O
A T I O E D Y S C O A C H D
T I L E T L L C H A R T E R
I C L Y J S L U F A R E H I
M K O P W S E O G Q I W B V
E E W M H A I R R G V L P E
S T R U M P I G K T A E S R
C S B B R U O T N N L G L O
H L E V A R T E K A Y N E U
O C C R O W D E D C L S T T
O Y N Y P U T Q T H T S I E
L I T E T X Q K H A X E S X
O I F S B X E B T N V N N I
C J D P U B L I C G C I A T
A V A B T S O C N E W O R K
L M O H A N D L E P I R T P
```

Solution on Page 302

CASUAL	MEETING
CHAT	MENU
COFFEE	MODEST
DELI	NOISY
DESSERT	PATIO
DINE	PEOPLE
DISHES	PIE
DRINKS	PLATES
EAT	RELAX
FAMILIAR	SALAD
FARE	SERVER
FILLING	SIP
FOOD	SMALL
FRESH	SOUP
FRIENDS	STEW
GRILLED	TABLE
HOMEY	TALK
INFORMAL	WAITER
LIVELY	
LOCAL	
LOUNGE	
LUNCH	

```
T N P G N C F K C D B F M L
G A S R W H L O F Y S I O N
L A B E P A T I O Z E U D X
I X F L T T I P Y D N R E L
K C W A E S H T L G I H S P
S I P X M Q K Y E A D O T U
G N I L L I F N V R T M N O
C S E P D E L L I R G E K S
G D D E E T H I L R M Y S Y
C J I N F O R M A L D H E Z
Q I L S E F P E E R U C C W
F R E S H I O L S E A N R W
A S E R V E R C E S T N C X
N T L L A M S F U S E I P H
Q L A F B F L A C O L D N B
M I L E D A L A S T E W J G
```

Solution on Page 302

ABROAD

ADVENTURE

BEDS

BUDGET

BUNK

CHEAP

CLEAN

COT

CULTURE

DORMITORY

EXPLORE

FOREIGN

FRIENDS

GROUP

HOMESICK

HOTEL

INN

LANGUAGE

LOUNGE

MEAL

NETWORK

OVERNIGHT

PEOPLE

PLACES

PRIVATE

PROGRAMS

RENT

ROOMS

SAFE

SECURE

SHARE

SOCIALIZE

STORAGE

STUDY

TEENAGERS

TOUR

TRAVEL

TRIP

VISIT

WALK

```
P X M P I R T N Y D U T S C
P T R A V E L O U N G E B H
T H O E R U T L U C D G U E
N P O F G R O U P R A D F A
E W M M O A K L T T O U M P
R E S I E R U E H R R B E L
A L R B O S E G M W B K A A
H P C W U N I I N N A E L C
S O T U A N T C G A S S D E
T E T G R O K Y K N L M Y S
N P E E R U T N E V D A E T
L R V Y L W S D N E I R F O
S O C I A L I Z E J B G A R
H B E D S I K L A W Q O S A
O I A N N I H S E C U R E G
O P R I V A T E R O L P X E
```

Solution on Page 303

AIRPORT

BEACH

BREAK

BUSY

CANDY

CARRY

COLD

COMMUTE

COOKIES

CROWDS

DELAY

DINNER

DRIVE

FAMILY

FLY

GETAWAY

GIFT

HOLLY

HOME

HUGS

HURRIED

ICE

LUGGAGE

PEACE

PILLOW

PLAN

PRESENT

REUNION

ROADS

ROUTE

SALE

SANTA

SKIING

SLEIGH

SNOW

STARS

STRESS

TRAIN

VISIT

WINTER

```
E P S M H T G Q G N I I K S
W L R E N N I D E I R R U H
S O L Y D N A C T C K Y X O
D A N A L P C R A V I S I T
S H S S Y I O S W G I S T A
S J Y L F P M R A K A E R B
G V L E R Q M A Y R U R A M
U O S I C Z U T F O E T I D
H W A G U S T S M U G S N P
M I N H H N E P N T G S D E
Y N T C E G D I E E J D E A
K T A S A E O L K V G W L C
I E E G U N M L O O I O A E
B R G I S D A O R C O R Y Y
P U Q F O N I W H A R C D P
L H X T W Q L O O Y S U B M
```

Solution on Page 303

AIRLINE

AIRPORT

ARRIVAL

CAREER

CLIENT

COMPANY

CONTACTS

DINNER

DISCUSS

DOMESTIC

FARE

FLY

GOALS

GROUP

HOTEL

JOURNEY

LAPTOP

LUGGAGE

MANAGE

MEETING

MERGER

NOTES

PARTNER

PEERS

PHONE

PILLOW

PITCH

PLAN

QUICK

REPORT

RUSH

SALES

SEMINAR

SUIT

TALK

TASKS

TICKET

TRAVEL

VENDORS

WORK

```
L S K S A T R O P E R G E P
K N S U I T E K C I T W L I
I S R D M Y L F G O A L S Y T
W X E A R E G A G G U L R C
R E N N I D N F N L E T O H
C D E A T O S R O D N E V W
M O N G T R E P U O R G A T
L M N E Y N A P M O C W R A
R E S T I M M P V J J O R L
E S E L A S E M I N A R I K
E T R E C C E N O H P K V C
R I E V F L T R O P R I A I
A C G A H D I S C U S S L U
C K R R S E N E X M K N H Q
T E E T U M G L N A L P I V
Q D M S R E E P O T P A L M
```

Solution on Page 303

AGRICULTURE

ANN ARBOR

APPLE BLOSSOM

BATTLE CREEK

FLINT

FORD

GENERAL MOTORS

GRAND RAPIDS

GREAT LAKES

LAKE ERIE

LANSING

LIVONIA

MARQUETTE PARK

MITTEN STATE

MOUNT ARVON

NOVI

PAINTED TURTLE

PETUNIAS

PONTIAC

ROYAL OAK

SOUTHFIELD

TAYLOR

TROY

WAYNE STATE

WESTLAND

WHITE PINE

WYOMING

```
E M I T T E N S T A T E S D
P A I N T E D T U R T L E N
O R Y S E K A L T A E R G A
N Q D Y Y M P T L S R S W L
T U B L O O P N T A O A A T
I E G A R U L I A I Y N Y S
A T R K T N E L Y N A N N E
C T A E D T B F L U L A E W
G E N E R A L M O T O R S H
N P D R O R O E R E A B T I
I A R I F V S S C P K O A T
S R A E C O S X T R V R T E
N K P A I N O V I L E Z E P
A P I W Y O M I N G W E K I
L O D L E I F H T U O S K N
A S S A G R I C U L T U R E
```

Solution on Page 303

BAREFOOT

BEACH

BOAT

CASTLE

CLAMS

CLIFFS

COAST

CONCHES

CRAB

DOCK

DOLPHINS

DUNES

FISH

FOAM

HARBOR

HOME

HOTEL

OCEAN

PALMS

PAVILION

PIER

PORT

RESORT

RETREAT

ROCK

SALTY

SAND

SEAFOOD

SEAGULLS

SEAWEED

SHELL

SHIP

SHORE

SUNSET

SURF

TIDE

TOWEL

VIEW

WAVE

WHALES

Solution on Page

```
R E S O R T S E L A H W R I
S A N D P V M H L X I W I R
H S I F O S L D I T D O C K
S S H O R E A V E P S L O Z
T L P E T E P L H E A A N G
A O L N S W I D T M W O C S
E V O U H S U P S Y I A H U
R T D F G N B D M L C I E N
T O V E E A M O I O R E S S
E W B S H R E V A P A D E E
R E L R C V A S I T B Z A T
N L O L A P T B F E E N F I
Z C S W E H C I M F W M O D
K K Z K B H X G A V I G O E
J T T Z R S S H O T E L D H
O K N O M S U R F N A E C O
```

Solution on Page 304

ACCELERATOR

AIR

ALIGNMENT

ANTIFREEZE

BATTERY

BELTS

BRAKES

CARBURETOR

CHECK LIGHTS

CLEANER

EMISSIONS

ENGINE

FILTER

FLUID

FRESHENER

FUEL

GASKETS

GASOLINE

HOSE

IGNITION

INSPECTION

MILEAGE

MOTOR

OIL

POLISH

RADIATOR

ROTATE

ROTORS

SERVICE

STEERING

SUSPENSION

TANK

TRANSMISSION

VACUUM

WAX

WIPERS

```
I M U U C A V D I U L F L K
N R O T O R S T E E R I N G
S T H G I L K C E H C A A A
P Q R E T L I F S S T S E S
E E C A R B U R E T O R N K
C M C W N E A M I L E A G E
T I F I L S O T I E Z J I T
I S M P V T M N T B E S N S
O S L E O R E I C E E K E B
N I L R E N E H S E R F S Q
N O I S N E P S U S F Y O S
X N O I T I N G I A I R H E
A S A C C E L E R A T O R K
W P E A L I G N M E N T N A
C L E A N E R A D I A T O R
P O L I S H E T A T O R J B
```

Solution on Page 304

AFTERNOON	RAT RACE
ARRIVAL	RIDE
BICYCLE	ROUTE
BIKE	SCHEDULE
BUS	SCHOOL
CAB	SHORT
CITY	STATION
COFFEE	STOPS
COMMUTER	STUDENTS
DAILY	SUBWAY
DRIVE	TAXI
EVENING	TICKET
FLY	TIME
FREEWAYS	TOWN
GAS	TRAIN
HOME	TRIP
JOB	WALK
LONG	WORK
MORNING	
NEWS	
PASSES	
RADIO	

Solution on P.

Commuting

```
C E D I R P J V J Y W Z W F
G X I A R R I V A L A O V V
T T D E E F F O C F E H R N
J I K F T M R U T S C O A K
O I L H U L I E B U A M L Y
B S A G M O R T E B R E S D
U S W K M N G S W W T L P P
S E H S O G N R N A A C O F
H T D O C G I U E Y R Y T T
Q I N R R H N N W O T C S K
R C T E I T E I S T U I T F
Z K P X D V V D N C R B A C
C E A A T U E U U R H A T F
I T I R O U T E D L O O I Y
T L I Y S E S S A P E M O N
Y P V S I C K Q E U A G N L
```

ADVENTURE

BUS

CAPITAL

CHAPERONE

CHILDREN

CITY HALL

CLASS

CULTURE

DRIVING

EXPLORE

FUN

GROUPS

HISTORY

INSIDE

JAUNT

JUNKET

LESSON

LISTEN

LUNCH

MONUMENT

MUSEUM

OPERA

OUTING

OUTSIDE

PLAN

SCHEDULE

SCHOOL

SCIENCE

SEEING

SHOW

SOUVENIR

STUDY

TEACHER

THEATER

TICKET

TOUR

TRAVEL

TRIPS

VISIT

ZOO

```
S E E I N G N I T U O O Z K
S C I E N C E E O H G K N B
T E A C H E R U T L U C O T
T H E A T E R M U S E U M R
E T O U T S I D E U I K E A
K I N S I D E S L G W L X V
N C A E O C P T N I X C P E
U K L N L U C I T Y H A L L
J E P A O U V O L A M C O E
A T S R H I D E P O E W R S
U S G C R U T E N E O F E S
N B N D S I R U H I R H U O
T U F T S O M U U C R A C N
L S U I N E Y R O T S I H S
A D V E N T U R E T R I P S
Y L A T I P A C W O H S H P
```

AIR	NASA
ALTITUDE	NAVIGATION
BALLOONING	OPERATION
BIRD	PASSENGER
BLIMP	PILOT
BOEING	PLANE
CARGO	ROCKET
COCKPIT	ROUTE
COMMERCIAL	SKY
DESIGN	SPACE
DEVELOPMENT	SPEED
ENGINE	TRANSPORT
FLY	TRAVEL
FUEL	WEATHER
GLIDER	WRIGHT
HELICOPTER	ZEPPELIN
HINDENBURG	
JET	
LIFT	
LINDBERGH	
MACH	
MILITARY	

```
T H G I R W H Q B S K Y G P
M G G Y B E T U O R P R D A
A R U R E H T A E W U A N S
C E E A E G C R I B O A C S
H B D T E N I G N E V O T E
Y D U I P M A E G I C O R N
L N T L G O D L G K G N O G
F I I I N N C A P R O I P E
Z L T M I G T I A I T L S R
S G L H N I T C L A E E N T
P L A L O S S R R E J P A R
E I P N O E L E U F H P R A
E D H I L D P M I L B E T V
D E V E L O P M E N T Z F E
D R I B A O R O C K E T I L
I G Q D B D T C A S A N L C
```

Solution on Page 305

ADAMS COUNTY

BAYARD

BEATRICE

BLAIR

CASS COUNTY

CHIMNEY ROCK

CONAGRA

CORNHUSKERS

DAKOTA CITY

DODGE COUNTY

GAGE COUNTY

GRAND ISLAND

GREAT PLAINS

HALL COUNTY

HOMESTEADERS

KEARNEY

LEXINGTON

LINCOLN

LOUP RIVER

NORTH PLATTE

OMAHA

OREGON TRAIL

SARPY COUNTY

SCOTTS BLUFF

SEWARD

WAHOO

YORK

```
O K G A G E C O U N T Y F K
R R C R E V I R P U O L F E
E O E H E S E W A R D E U A
G Y T Y I A Y H M I R X L R
O R T D T M T P I A A I B N
N C A N A N N P A L Y N S E
T O L N U K U E L B A G T Y
R R P L D O O O Y A B T T T
A N H O C I C T C R I O O N
I H T C O O S E A Y O N C U
L U R N N H M L G C P C S O
P S O I A G A A A D I R K C
V K N L G E D W H N O T A S
W E C I R T A E B A D D Y S
S R E D A E T S E M O H X A
U S Y T N U O C L L A H E C
```

Solution on Page 305

AREA

BEACH

BUS

CAMP

CHEAP

COSTLY

CROWDED

FAKE

FEE

FLASHY

FOOD

GIFT

GIMMICK

HANGOUT

HAUNT

HAVEN

HIDEOUT

HISTORY

HOTEL

HYPE

INN

JUNK

LODGE

LORE

MAP

MONEY

MOTEL

MUGS

PARK

POPULAR

REFUGE

REST

RETREAT

SHOP

SOUVENIR

SPA

TICKET

TOYS

TRIP

VISITORS

```
K S B Z I Q A Z P T R I P H
E A P B Q C V E G D O L N D
K H T U W N N I R T V Y T H
F M Q S O C M A S A R A S O
Y C O G E M O P M I E W E C
C R F T I R Q S N R T R R X
L E E C E A K E T J O O A H
E E K E T L V E U L W N R I
T B A D U U R R O D Y P F S
O K F D O P M K E S H L T T
H R H S G O T D D F A B I O
T A C C N P F X I S U K C R
M P V E A K I H H G N G K Y
A F Y E H E G Y V U T E E E
P O H S N I B P J M K G T J
Z C A M P D W E J M B I O T
```

Solution on Page 305

BENCHES

BUGS

CABIN

CAMPER

COOLERS

EAT

EXPLORE

FAMILY

FAUNA

FEE

FIRE

FISH

FLORA

FOOD

FRIENDS

FUN

GRILL

HIKE

LOGS

NATURE

OUTDOORS

PARK

PICNIC

RELAX

RESERVE

ROAST

RULES

RUSTIC

SITE

SLEEP

SONGS

SUNRISE

SUNSET

SWIM

TARP

TENT

THERMOS

TRAIL

TREES

WEEKEND

```
G L B R F D U C F L O R A M
I R F S C I N C I P A N V N
D L I A W T A E T T U P U R
D N B L C I R R K A S F I U
Q I S Y L I M A F E I U B L
N J P L S U N R I S E C R E
T A R P E C I Q H L M W S S
N P M I A E R O L P X E R G
E S W M N R P I T K H E O N
T E P D K E K H H C L F O O
R E S E R V E I N O S B D S
R R E U C R K E O H H G T D
K T T F M E B C T E S N U S
N A H O D L C Q A R T G O B
N W S R O A S T N I T I O C
A S J V N X D O O F Z N S L
```

Solution on Page 305

AFRICA	JOURNEY
AIRFARE	LONDON
AIRPORT	PACK
ASIA	PARIS
BAGS	RELAX
BEACH	RETREAT
BICYCLE	ROME
CRUISE	SAFARI
CUSTOMS	SKI
EUROPE	SPA
EXPLORE	SUN
FAMILY	SWIM
FERRY	TAN
FLIGHT	TENT
FRIENDS	TOUR
FUN	TRAIL
GOLF	TRIP
HAWAII	VISIT
HIKE	
HOLIDAY	
HOTEL	
ISLAND	

Solution on

```
Z A T E N T P T I S I V Z S
N V I U T M R O M E O K G J
I A S L O N D O N N H A S O
F F L I G H T B P A B I W U
P D N A L S I E W R B S E R
H U A E U E R A F R I A P N
F G T C I A I C K U C A O E
F O R R R I Q H P O Y H R Y
H L I U A L I A R T C O U V
V F P I F Z R S P A L L E G
L Z S S A I D D W P E I K H
O Z I E S F A N X I P D I Y
E E I R E T R E A T M A H N
Q F E R R Y L I M A F Y C X
R O T X A L E R C W E M J K
Q G S S W X N F T A B Z G U
```

Solution on Page 306

ANNUAL

BAMBOO

BEES

BIRDS

BLOOM

BUSH

CACTUS

CLIMATE

COLORS

CONIFER

EXHIBIT

EXOTIC

EXPLORE

FLORAL

FLOWER

FOREST

GREEN

HERB

IMPORT

LEAVES

LILAC

LOTUS

MOIST

NATIVE

ORCHID

PATHS

PEONY

PLANT

POLLEN

RARE

ROSE

SCENIC

SPROUT

TOUR

TRAILS

TREES

TULIP

VINES

WARM

WATER

Botanical Gardens

```
J B C Y D I H C R O M Q R H
Z C U P P L N E L L O P E S
C I N E C S W N X A N R T B
P K O R A O E A C P B E A O
C N P I L U T V R Y L X W K
Y E L F I T T B A M B O O X
X L A L L R S T R E G T R B
X H N O S A I U C M L I A E
R S T R U I O O N O C C X B
O U Y A T L M R Q O L H I I
S B M L C S R P B L I O G R
E S H T A P E S O B M X R D
N L S R C U R R I R A R E S
I P U E G A N T O T T V E M
V O I E E C O N I F E R N K
T V D S C B E N A T I V E A
```

Solution on Page 306

ADVENTURE

AGENT

BEACH

BREAK

CRUISE

CULTURE

DISCOVERY

DRIVE

ENJOY

EXCURSION

EXPLORE

FAMILY

FLY

FOOD

FRIENDS

FUN

GETAWAY

HIGHWAY

HIKING

HISTORY

JOURNEY

MOUNTAIN

MUSEUM

OUTINGS

PACK

PARADISE

PEOPLE

PLAN

RELAX

RESORT

SAFARI

SCHEDULE

SUITCASE

SUMMER

TOUR

TRAIN

TREK

TRIP

TROPICS

VIEWS

```
T K T R A I N A L P E M O B
X A L E R U O T U I U U P E
B E G C R U I S E E T M S A
H R D E X C U R S I O N W C
I B I N N R U U N U J U E H
S P S U U T M G N O S L I S
T L C F N O S T U S U K V A
O L O E R P A R A D I S E F
R G V R Q I N W E N T C R A
Y D E U N E E H G C C I O R
A S R T Y P C N K C A P L I
W U Y L A S D A D N S O P P
H M L U F W T R O S E R X I
G M F C O F A M I L Y T E R
I E L P O E P Y S V K E R T
H R X I D O Y O J N E J C U
```

Solution on Page 306

ANCHOR

AQUEDUCTS

BARGE

BOAT

CANOE

CAPTAIN

CARRIER

CATAMARAN

CHANNEL

DINGHY

DRIFT

ENGINE

FERRY

FLOAT

GONDOLA

KAYAK

LAKE

LINER

MOTOR

OCEAN

PADDLE

RAFT

RIVER

ROW

SAIL

SCHOONER

SEA

SHIP

SUBMARINE

SWIM

TANKER

TUNNELS

VOYAGE

WATER TAXI

WAVES

YACHT

```
C Z L C X W A J S H I P M C
S Y A M V W Z G S B O W W L
L E N G I N E L D D A P N Y
I C A Q U E D U C T S R P R
N D R I F T L X E O U R G R
E G A Y O V C R C D B O M E
R M M R Q A T E T C M H J F
E K A L P A A N H S A C J C
O R T T X N B O C L R N H K
T E A I F T P O A E I A W A
P I C D I N G H Y N N P A Y
N R E K N A T C X N E R V A
R R M O L I A S E U O I E K
C A G O N D O L A T P V S G
R C F L O A T B O A T E N D
J Z D T Z N C M I W S R O W
```

Solution on Page 306

CAMPING

CASINOS

CAVING

CHURCHILL

CLARK

DOUGLAS

EGAN RANGE

ELY

ESMERALDA

EUREKA

FALLON

FISHING

GAMBLING

GAMING

GOLD

HAWTHORNE

HIKING

HUMBOLDT

HUNTING

KINGSBURY

LANDER

LAS VEGAS

LINCOLN

LYON

MCGILL

MT GRAFTON

NYE

PARADISE

PERSHING

PIOCHE

RENO

TONOPAH

WASHOE

WHITE PINE

WINNEMUCCA

YERINGTON

```
F G N I K I H S A L G U O D
I C P H A P O N O T G Z G U
S A G E V S A L U N N N N L
H M D R J E E H C O I P I L
I P G L E E S H R H T S M I
N I A H A N U I S V N G A G
G N M E A R O R D N U N G C
E G B O C G E T E A H I E M
N G L H C P O M F K R V N T
O C I S U E Y L S A A A I D
L L N A M L A N D E R C P L
L A G W E G N A R N A G E O
A R L E N R O H T W A H T B
F K K I N G S B U R Y E I M
Y Y E R I N G T O N Y M H U
L Y O N W N L O C N I L W H
```

Solution on Page 307

ANCIENT	LAVISH
ASIA	LUXURY
CASTLE	MANOR
CENTER	MOAT
DECOR	OLD
DUKE	ORNATE
EARL	POWER
EMPIRE	PRINCE
ESTATE	QUEEN
EUROPE	REGAL
FAMILY	ROOMS
FANCY	ROYAL
FRANCE	RULER
GARDEN	STYLE
GRAND	SULTAN
GUARD	THRONE
HALL	TOWER
HEIR	VAST
HOME	
HUGE	
KING	
LARGE	

```
W P H B H C Y R O Y A L G H
R P Y X D K V B E G U H U G
U K O U F A N C Y T R S N U
P H Q U E E N E A E N A A A
O H S I V A L O U S Y E N R
L U X U R Y H R F T T Y C D
D W U F T P O N H A L L I M
C H X S R P M A W T H I E L
F L A I E G E T N E M M N R
L V E K W T T E E A P A T R
F H U M O A T P D I T F Q O
G D C R P E N O R H T L Z O
U M W W S G A E A I S A U M
P R E L U R G R G G N I K S
W W R O N A M I L R O C E D
Z W A T L L L Y K U T O W E R
```

Solution on Page 307

ARTERY

ATTENDANT

BALLAST

BRAKE

CAR

CHEF

COMMUTE

CONDUCTOR

COOK

CROSSING

DIESEL

DINING

ELECTRIC

ENGINE

FREIGHT

GOODS

GUEST

HAUL

JUNCTION

LIGHTS

LINE

LOAD

MAID

PASS

POINTS

PORTER

RAILS

ROUTE

SEAT

SIGNAL

SLEEPERS

SPIKE

STATION

STEAM

SWITCH

TICKET

TIES

TRACK

WHEELS

WHISTLE

```
P C P E T U O R L O A D C E
A H C T I W S T A T I O N B
S T E A M A I D G I M I W W
S N S A R T E R Y M L O H T
D A S A E O O K U T S S E R
Z D D S L L T T A R A K E A
T N O I R L E C J R C E L C
E E O P E E A C U I B E S K
Z T G N O S P B T D G T J L
G T R T D R E E C R N X U U
U A W H I S T L E I I O N A
E N I G N E L E O L S C C H
S T H G I L S P R I S U T W
T O L A N G I S C O O K I G
J N Q R G T H G I E R F O P
S P I K E D F F F E H C T N R
```

Solution on Page 307

ALIGNMENT

AUTOMATIC

BATTERY

BELT

BODY

BRAKES

CLUTCH

DIPSTICK

ENGINE

EXHAUST

EXTERIOR

FIX

FLUID

GARAGE

GASKET

GREASE

HOOD

HOSE

HUB

IGNITION

INHIBITOR

INTERIOR

JACK

LIGHTS

LUBRICANT

MECHANIC

MOTOR

MUFFLER

OIL

PAINT

RADIATOR

SHOP

STARTER

SWITCH

TIRE

TOOLS

TORQUE

WARRANTY

WIRES

WRENCH

```
E S O H U B U F I X H O O D
H Y R E T T A B L N C R T A
X T O R Q U E I D U T A L T
M O T O R H O N I T I R E N
E W A H O C N H P N W D B I
N O I T I N G I S A S T R A
G T D C R E G B T C T E A P
I N A R E R R I I I H K K K
N E R O T W E T C R G S E C
E M B I N T A O K B I A S A
R N O R I M S R W U L G T J
W G D E O M E U X L D A A P
I I Y T N A R R A W U R R O
R L U X C L U T C H M A T H
E A M E C H A N I C X G E S
S L O O T V M U F F L E R T
```

Solution on Page 307

ALERTS

ANNOUNCE

BULLETIN

BUSINESS

CAMPAIGN

CHURCH

CITY

CLEVER

COLORFUL

CONTACT

DIGITAL

DRIVERS

ENDORSE

EVENTS

EXPOSURE

FOOD

FUEL

HOTELS

HYPE

IMAGES

INFORM

LOCAL

LOOK

MESSAGE

MOVIES

NOTICE

PICTURE

PITCH

PLUG

PROMOTE

READ

RETAIL

ROADWAY

SELL

SERVICES

SHOW

SLOGAN

STORE

TOUT

VISUAL

```
W O H S L O C A L A U S I V
D U C U F D I G I T A L E T
E P T O H E D T S C H O R T
C P I Y L R U E T A E G O H
I A P C I O C Q N T X A T B
T E M V T I R N L N P N S D
O E E P V U O F F O O D E A
N R T R A U R P U C S C I E
S M E O N I T E L L U B V R
Z S O C M K G R M L R J O S
C L E S R O D N E V E A M S
P H I N F O R M S V D U T E
E P U A I L O P S W E N F G
A L E R T S H C A E E L U A
L Y T I C E U Y G V L L C M
S L E T O H R B E W P L M I
```

Solution on Page 308

BATH	PORCH
BED	QUAINT
CAMP	QUIET
CANOE	RENTAL
COT	RETREAT
FAMILY	REUNION
FIRE	RICKETY
FISHING	RIVER
FOREST	RURAL
GETAWAY	RUSTIC
GUEST	SECURE
HOME	SERENE
HOUSE	SHELTER
HUNTING	SIMPLE
INTIMATE	SMALL
ISOLATED	SUMMER
KITCHEN	TRIP
LAKE	VIEWS
LOG	
MOUNTAIN	
NATURE	
PEACEFUL	

Cabins

```
P M A C R S R S B R H C R P
T V Y I E E E A E H P I R T
C S V R T C T U V V C T O C
C E E L U H N R I K R S S Q
R N E R Z I T S E U G U U E
E H E G O L N T W A E R M U
S O A N P F Y T S D T F M D
P U T F E G D L I F A B E D
O S N I A T N U O M W T R T
R E I S C M P I S C A N O E
C M A H E Y I I T L Y T E I
H O U I F T M L O N A R E U
D H Q N U P A S Y K U K H Q
C Y B G L R I K I T C H E N
A T I E U P U L A T N E R H
S F I R E M D N L L A M S S
```

Solution on Page 308

PUZZLES • 79

AUTONOMY

BNU TOWER

BRIDGES

CANTONESE

CASINOS

CAUSEWAY

CHEOC VAN

CHINA

COLONY

COTAI

CULTURE

GRAND PRIX

HAC SA

HOSPITALITY

MACANESE

MACAU TOWER

MANUFACTURING

PATACA

PENHA HILL

PORTUGAL

SANDS MACAO

SOVEREIGNTY

SUBTROPICAL

TAXIS

TOURISTS

TRADING PORT

TYPHOONS

VENETIAN MACAU

WYNN MACAU

```
P O C H I N A V C O E H C Y
A M A C A U T O W E R O A A
T S A N D S M A C A O S S W
A P E N H A H I L L X P C E
C F Y C U L T U R E L I A S
A G T A G F R S I X A T H U
V E N E T I A N M A C A U A
I S G S S A D C A B I L X C
S T I E N U I C T N P I I P
E S E N O T N A C U O T R O
G I R A O O G S O T R Y P R
D R E C H N P I L O T I D T
I U V A P O O N O W B A N U
R O O M Y M R O N E U T A G
B T S S T Y T S Y R S O R A
W Y N N M A C A U A F C G L
```

Solution on Page 308

ANCHORS

BEDDING

CANOE

CLASSICS

COMPASS

CONCEPTS

CONTESTS

COVERS

CRUISERS

CUSTOM

DEALERS

DEBUT

DECK

DINGHIES

DISPLAY

ENGINE

EXHIBIT

FENDER

HARBOR

JET

KAYAK

KIT

LEISURE

MARINE

MODELS

MOTOR

OARS

PADDLES

PONTOON

POWER

PUMP

SAIL

SEAT

SHIPS

SONAR

TICKETS

TOURISM

TRADE

WOODEN

YACHTS

Solution on Page

```
O Z H A R B O R E D N E F G
K A N Z M S I R U O T E J S
M A R E W O P C O V E R S R
O Y Y S G A J T I B I H X E
D S C A D N N E P U M P E L
E T D D K O I S R O H C N A
L P L Y P U S D T U R T G E
S E Y A C H T S D U S T I D
S C T L I K U T I E Y I N K
A N I P F C D S N N B C E F
P O S S T E E E G I A K D L
M C Z I S R C T H R T E O N
O U A D S A K N I A A T O Q
C R A N O S L O E M Q S W D
X M O T O R P C S A I L L T
Y W T U B E D A R T A E S V
```

Solution on Page 308

AMAZING

BABY

BARNACLE

BEAUTY

BEHAVIOR

BELUGA

BLUE

BOAT

CAMERA

CRESTING

DIVE

FEED

FERRY

GIANT

GROUPS

GUIDE

HABITAT

HERD

HUMPBACK

ICE

JACKET

JUMP

KILLER

LUNGING

MORNING

NATURE

OCEAN

ORCA

PATIENCE

SEA

SHIP

SPLASH

SPRAY

SWIM

TOUR

VIDEO

VIEWING

WAITING

WATER

WAVES

Go Whale Watching

```
E Z G Z M N W B N D M P M E
R O K W L Y T A O B F O V B
Y N V J U M P B V E C I E A
G R O U P S O Y R E D I U G
T N E E P G O R A R S S L U
R S I L D R Y N N O H W B L
U E A W C I P A T I E N C E
W S T A E A V K P V N K T B
H A M A Z I N G C A C G K E
R R I D W R V R B H G C G R
G E Y T U A E B A E A N J U
Y M L O I S S H A B I T A T
V A T L T N E P P G N I C A
O C R I I R G M N A G C K N
U K N P D K U U I L D E E F
V G A E S H L G M I W S T D
```

Solution on Page 309

PUZZLES • **85**

ARCH

BAR

BEAM

BOND

BROOKLYN

CABLE

CARS

CEMENT

CONCRETE

CONDUIT

GIRDER

HIGH

LAND

LINK

LOG

OVER

PASSAGE

PATH

PEACE

PIERS

RAINBOW

RIVER

ROAD

ROPE

SCENIC

SPAN

STEEL

STONE

STREET

STRONG

TAMPICO

TOWER

TRANSIT

TRAVEL

TRESTLE

TRUSS

VIADUCT

WALK

WATER

WOODEN

```
H R Q D A U D P N G F U L T
W P O U T R E S T L E O Q T
O X T H R A T N C T G M H H
D E Q O C D E I E I A L F W
J N P E W M N R S E S E G O
C E F D E E C A B N S V N C
T Z T C C N R B L P A A O O
A I R S O Y K L A W P R R C
M T U C F L W N U G I T T I
P O S D E K W O S I Y C S E
I U S E N O T S O R U T E H
C W T C B O C D O D E L G T
O S A N O R C A A E E I D A
E L I T V B D I R R H N P P
C A B L E G V T C S O K D M
R E V I R R S Z H B N C C V
```

Solution on Page 309

BOOKS

BORDER

BREAK

CAMPING

CITY

COOLER

DETOUR

DINER

DRIVE

EXPLORE

FAMILY

FOOD

FUEL

GETAWAY

GPS

HIGHWAY

HOTEL

LOST

MAP

MOTEL

MUSIC

RADIO

REST

RIDE

ROAD

ROUTE

SEAT

SIGNS

SNACKS

SONGS

SPEED

STATE

STOP

TIME

TOWN

TOYS

TRAVEL

TRIP

TRUNK

VIEWS

```
X L C D P L E D K N W O T S
L B O M O T E L E U F A K R
V O O A K T C V O E E A E S
F I L O O N F T A S E S T S
F C E U K I U P D R T A D N
A T R W D S D R B Y T G B D
T I M E S U I A T E N X I M
U D E I D V Y D R I Y N C H
P P D V E R O L P X E Q I A
S A I C C Y O M I R Q G T X
T M R O A D A B R M H P Y R
O M U S I C Y W T W A S D O
P S O N G S K C A N S F N F
W K Y Y X P Z Y E T U O R H
P B E O B M N H O T E L O V
F K K U T Y R I A S I G N S
```

Solution on Page 309

ACTION

BOOKS

CAMPING

CLIMB

CRUISE

DESERT

DIVE

EXPEDITION

EXPLORING

FUN

GAMES

GEOCACHE

GPS

HIKE

HUNT

JUNGLE

KAYAKING

MISSION

MOVIES

OCEAN

PADDLING

PARACHUTE

QUEST

RAFTING

RISK

ROPES

RUNNING

SAFARI

SAIL

SCARY

SCUBA

SHIP

SURFING

SWIM

TRAVEL

TREK

VALOR

VISIT

VOLCANO

WILDLIFE

```
J L G U N T S E U Q C K M C
G D Z O O P S U D E S E R T
V E M N I E A G N I F R U S
I L O A T T I D R Z W R N M
S G V C C U L D D T O D N I
I N I L A H E F I L D L I W
T U E O C C N K A V I G N S
R J S V Y A H V I H E N G C
E U K S E R M E N H G I G U
K R O C E A L P O N I R G B
I T O E X P E D I T I O N A
G R B O S N O K S N X L I D
N A A M U I A R S U G P T J
G V M F I Y U P I H S X F E
E E G E A L G R M X Y E A Z
I L W K S S C W C S C A R Y
```

Solution on Page 309

AMERICA

AREA

BASKETBALL

BUTLER

CARDINAL

COLTS

CORN

CROSSROADS

ELKHART

EVANSVILLE

FARMING

FOOTBALL

FORT WAYNE

GARY

HOOSIER

ILLINOIS

INDIANS

LAFAYETTE

LAKES

MAP

MIDWEST

MUNCIE

NOTRE DAME

OHIO

PACERS

PEONY

PURDUE

RACES

SOUTH BEND

SPEEDWAY

STEEL

TECUMSEH

TERRITORY

TRAVEL

TULIP TREE

UNIVERSITY

USA

WABASH

```
P E L L A B T O O F K W T E
A I Y E V A N S V I L L E T
C C R O S S R O A D S I C T
E N O E S K G S E K A L U E
R U T L P E A R E A C L M Y
S M I K E T R N Q O I I S A
G R R H E B Y O L P R N E F
N E R A D A M T T D E O H A
I I E R W L S R N P M I A L
M S T T A L E E T S A S U R
R O R O Y E B D R A C E S E
A O I N U H C A R D I N A L
F H O D T P A M I D W E S T
O E R U N I V E R S I T Y U
P U O L E V A R T C O R N B
P S N A I D N I H S A B A W
```

Solution on Page 310

BALLOON	RUN
BICYCLE	SAIL
BIKE	SCOOTER
BOAT	SHIP
BUS	SHUTTLE
CAR	SKIS
DOGSLED	SUBWAY
DRIVE	SWIM
FEET	TAXI
FERRY	TRICYCLE
FLY	TROLLEY
FREIGHT	UNICYCLE
GONDOLA	VAN
HIKE	VEHICLE
HORSE	VESPA
JET	WAGON
JOG	WALK
MONORAIL	YACHT
PLANE	
RAILROAD	
RIDE	
ROCKET	

```
M I W S P E B G V X Z D D R
R X R N K I H O N H W A D D
X A E L C I H E V O O O B M
T T T D K U S S O R G I J F
A R O E I L N A L S K A E H
O M O N O R A I L E U R W E
B C C L T C A E C O R B A E
M A S B L R D B R Y D F L Y
Y P U H H E I I P U C N K P
L Z B T U T Y C R R N L O U
J I W F H T H Y Y A O A E G
P L A N E G T C V C O P V W
I J Y S S E I L A D L S I L
L M L G O J T E E Y L E R N
W M F T E K C O R O A V D O
F N J T F N O I D F B H J B
```

Solution on Page 310

APPLICATOR

BLUSH

BOBBY PINS

BRONZER

BRUSH

CLIPPERS

COMB

CONCEALER

COTTON BALLS

CREAM

CURLER

FOUNDATION

GLOSS

LASHES

LINER

LIP BALM

LIPSTICK

LOTION

MAKEUP

MASCARA

MIRROR

MOISTURIZER

NAIL POLISH

PENCIL

PERFUME

POWDER

PRIMER

REMOVER

SANITIZER

SHADOW

TISSUE

TWEEZERS

WIPES

```
V B N O I T A D N U O F Y C
Q R O C P F W O D A H S O R
S O I U U N P E R F U M E B
E N T R E V O M E R B N A L
P Z O L K I M C O Z I P R U
I E L E A R H L L L E K A S
W R A R M E S S A X L R C H
V E P E X Z I N S B I E S S
L L P D L I L I H S P Z A U
K A L W E R O P E R S I M R
P E I O U U P Y S E T T L B
R C C P S T L B Z P I I I G
I N A U S S I B M P C N C L
M O T F I I A O V I K A N O
E C O T T O N B A L L S E S
R O R R I M A E R C Q F P S
```

Solution on Page 310

AIRPORT	PASSPORT
ARRIVAL	PLANE
BORDER	RAILWAY
BUS	RELAX
COUNTRY	SHIP
CRUISE	SHOPPING
CUISINE	SIGHTS
CULTURE	SOUVENIR
CUSTOMS	SUBWAY
EXPLORE	TAXI
FLYING	TICKETS
FOREIGN	TOUR
GUIDE	TRAIN
HOSTEL	TRIP
HOTEL	VILLAGE
JOURNEY	VISIT
JUNKET	VOYAGE
LANGUAGE	WALKING
LEARN	
LODGING	
LUGGAGE	
PACK	

```
G S I G H T S T E K C I T C
P T Y T I Y H N C G E V U E
I N A I R P O R T G E I F D
H I W Y Y I P A T N S L L I
S A B K R A P E K I M L Y U
T R U Q C T I L N K O A I G
I T S K U F N E E L T G N P
S R O L L L G U R A S E G L
I O U U T A I I O W U D N A
V P V G U V E X L C C H I N
N S E G R I R A P P O C G E
X S N A E R O T X T T R D Z
A A I G D R F Y E N R U O J
L P R E R A I L W A Y I L O
E G A Y O V N R L E T S O H
R U O T B U S J U N K E T Z
```

Solution on Page 310

ARCTIC

BARREN

BEAR

BRUSH

CANYON

CLIMB

COBRA

DEATH

DESERT

DRY

FOREST

HEAT

HILLS

JACKAL

JUNGLE

LION

LONELY

LOST

MONKEY

MOSS

OASIS

OPEN

PLAIN

PREY

PYTHON

REGION

RESCUE

ROCK

SAND

SEARCH

SNAKE

SWAMP

TIGER

TRACK

TREES

VAST

VINE

WATER

WILD

ZEBRA

```
J B L Q W L O N E L Y N U I
P S S Y E K N O M T E Y X E
S E I S D P E Y A R L I O N
L R S E V L L N R E G S E I
L E A A E A A A C S N E U V
I T O R K I B C T E U E Y C
H A Y C A N T S I D J R F N
U W A H N N E K C A R T J I
F J R N S R J D J R S E L V
J P B N O H T Y P A U C B J
H I E F E I I R V C L C F C
F P Z A P G G A S I O O F Z
O N T M I R E E M B Q K S K
H Y T Q O L R B R U S H P T
W N R C U S W A M P R E Y G
X A K D N A S D L I W F B W
```

Solution on Page 311

BAHT

BANG NA

BANGKOK NOI

BUENG KUM

CAPITAL

CHATUCHAK

CHOM THONG

COUPS

DIN DAENG

DON MUEANG

EXOTIC

GIANT SWING

HUAI KHWANG

KHAN NA YAO

KHLONG SAN

LAK SI

LAT KRABANG

LAT PHRAO

MIN BURI

NONG CHOK

NONG KHAEM

PATHUM WAN

PHAYA THAI

PRAWET

RAT BURANA

SATHON

SIAM

SUAN LUANG

THAILAND

THUNG KHRU

WAT ARUN

YAN NAWA

```
T A L A T P H R A O T L I L
D E G N A U L N A U S O A T
Y O W I R U B N I M N T W H
A D N A L I A H T K K I K U
N N U M R R H J O R C A A N
N O R H U P T K A L A H H G
A H A B G E G B S A P T C K
W T T Y G N A W H K I A U H
A A A B A N I N E S T Y T R
R S W B G N F W G I A A A U
D I N D A E N G S N L H H S
N A W M U H T A P T A P C I
B N A S G N O L H K N B C A
K O H C G N O N G K H A E M
B U E N G K U M E X O T I C
U S P U O C H O M T H O N G
```

Solution on Page 311

ADVENTURE	PRISTINE
AFFLUENCE	PRIVATE
AGENCY	QUALITY
BEACH	RELAX
BLISS	RESORT
BUTLER	RICHNESS
CATERED	SERVICE
CLASS	SKI
COMFORT	SPA
COSTLY	STAR
CRUISE	STEAK
ENJOY	SUITE
FAMOUS	TROPICS
FANCY	UNIQUE
FLAIR	VACATION
HOTEL	VILLA
INDULGE	WEALTHY
JET	YACHT
LIMO	
LUSH	
PARADISE	
PERKS	

```
M K Y A C H T A L L I V M S
C L R A T S E T A V I R P T
V I R Y O J N E H C A E B E
M M Q U A L I T Y N E S E A
C O M F O R T S B C U O P K
P A R A D I S E I L Q R E L
B K F R Y E I V J E I T R I
U E V F N D R P C G N S K H
T E A H L E P L A L U S S W
L S C B S U E G R U A U D E
E I A C A T E R E D L S H A
R U T N O N T N S N A P S L
H R I H C A I S C I P O R T
R C O Y E R U T N E V D A H
F A N C Y I S M C O S T L Y
S U O M A F L A I R E L A X
```

Solution on Page 311

BATHROOM	RESTROOM
BEVERAGES	RURAL
BLOWOUT	SEATS
BREAK	SEMI
BROCHURES	SHADE
CARS	SIGNS
CRUISING	SLEEP
DINING	SNACKS
DRINKS	STAND
EXIT	TABLE
EXPRESSWAY	TIRES
FOOD	TOW
FREEWAY	TRASH
GAS	TREES
HIGHWAY	TRUCKS
MAP	WALK
PARK	WASHROOM
PEACEFUL	WATER
PETS	
PLAZA	
REFUEL	
RELAX	

Rest Stop

```
S K R A P W M K K L A W G Q
R N L L W S I G N S J A H K
A W A E K C W V E X I T F A
C Z R C B L O W O U T E R E
A M U Y K T A F O Y J R E R
S R R K R S E G A R E V E B
T E D A H S U W S E M I W E
A I S R R E S T R O O M A L
N H O P C S T A E S O M Y B
D O E S E R U H C O R B A A
M T D R K A U I Z I H D W T
S S P O X N C I S K T I H I
C X L A O P I E S X A N G R
E Y L E U F E R F I B I I E
O E U M E R V Q D U N N H S
R Q W O T P A M R G L G A S
```

ACCOUNT

ADVENTURE

CHRONICLE

CITIES

COUNTRIES

CUISINE

CULTURE

DISCOVER

EVENT

EXPLORE

FAIRS

FILM

FOOD

GEOGRAPHY

JOURNAL

LEARN

LECTURE

MAP

MEMORIES

MOVIE

NARRATE

NATIVES

NATURE

PEOPLE

PHOTOS

PICTURES

PLAN

RECORD

SCHEDULE

SIGHTS

SLIDE

SOUNDS

STORY

TALK

TEACH

TOUR

TOWNS

TRACK

VIDEO

VOYAGE

```
N S O T O H P D O O F V L Y
N A V I D E O S E V I T A N
L R L F O X N A R R A T E T
A P A P I P S O U N D S A G
N D L E S L Q V T J E L V E
R E V V L O M J L R K E L O
U P S E I R T N U O C C A G
O A K N N E A T C E I T K R
J M S T G T C Z I N W U T A
N E T A U I U V O I G R E P
T M Y R P S O R O S I E A H
U O E C A M H S E I T I C Y
V R E V O C S I D U L H H R
S I G H T S K R E C O R D O
V E D I L S N W O T R U O T
T S C H E D U L E F A I R S
```

Solution on Page 312

BAKERY

BATTER

BEAR CLAW

BOX

CAKE

CHOCOLATE

CINNAMON

COFFEE

CRULLER

CUSTARD

DESSERT

DOUGH

DUNKIN

FILLED

FLOUR

FOOD

FRESH

FRIED

FROSTED

FRUIT

GLAZE

HOLE

ICED

ICING

JELLY

KRISPY KREME

MAPLE

NUTS

PASTRY

PLAIN

POWDER

RING

ROUND

SHOP

SNACK

STORE

SUGAR

SWEET

TREAT

YEAST

Grab a Doughnut

```
I S R E D W O P L A I N R A
Q W F E L P A M P D R B O X
J E K R I S P Y K R E M E R
Y E A S T O R E N A L I A S
N T L R F L O U R Z L G R K
A N Y L F Z T C D N U O R F
E P A R Y S L H U S R I B S
L R E T T A B O G S C F A H
O S Z R W S L C S U T X K O
H G A E E F F O C N O A E P
L U L A D E L L I F A D R F
G T G T N O M A N N I C Y D
N I K N U D E T S O R F K O
I U C O I K D E S S E R T O
C R M E A R V W M Y K N O F
I F S C D Q N Z B U O F Z S
```

Solution on Page 312

PUZZLES • **111**

CAMERA

CAPSIZE

CURRENT

DANGER

DARING

DRIFT

DROPS

FALLS

FAST

FLIP

FUN

GRADES

GUIDE

IMPACT

JACKET

KAYAK

LAUGH

OAR

PADDLE

PICNIC

RAFT

RAPIDS

RISKY

RIVER

ROCKS

ROUGH

SCREAM

SPLASH

SPORT

SUIT

SUMMER

SWIM

THRILL

TRIP

TUBE

TUMBLE

VEST

WATER

WET

WILD

```
A P X S P I R T F I R D G P
E Z H G U O R S U I T E W L
F B Y F T M Q M S M R M S U
A A U S F Q M K T A B F C D
M O S T Z U Y E P S O L R R
P B F T A G N I R A D U E O
F A I H Q D D H E L D D A P
R A J R L S G Z G O G R M S
O F L I P U R R N R A O I E
C K W L A A T C A P M I W Z
K I A L S E S D D R R M S I
S S N Y K W E E T E E N U S
H L P C A S V R V F D M F P
Y U A T I K O I L T Y I A A
N J E R F P R T N E R R U C
L R P C S K X P P A K O K G
```

Solution on Page 312

AMENITIES

ANNIVERSARY

ANTIQUE

BED

BOOKS

BREAKFAST

CHARM

COFFEE

COUNTRY

COUPLES

COZY

EXPENSIVE

FRIENDLY

GARDEN

GUESTS

HISTORIC

HOLIDAY

HOME

HOST

INN

LOCALS

MEMORABLE

OVERNIGHT

OWNER

PERSONAL

PRIVATE

PROPRIETOR

RATES

RESERVATION

ROMANTIC

ROOMS

STAFF

SUITE

THEMES

TOURISTS

UNIQUE

VACATION

WELCOME

```
B N T P V S Y A D I L O H F
O O O H R L E R G A R D E N
O I U I S O C I T N A M O R
K T R S T C P N T N H N X S
S A I T A A O R B I U O M A
E C S O F L V S I V N O S G
T A T R F S E R L E O E C T
A V S I F L R A E R T E M S
R Y A C P R N T X S P O P A
C Z A U E O I H P A E M R F
O O O N S S G E E R M R I K
F C W R T U H M N Y O A V A
F O E S U I T E S D C H A E
E P E M O H Q S I B L C T R
E U N I Q U E U V H E Y E B
G E L B A R O M E M W D M C
```

Solution on Page 312

ACCIDENTS

ADVISORY

BLIZZARD

BLOCKED

BOOKED

CLEAR

CLOSURE

CONGESTED

CRAMMED

CROWDS

DELAY

DETOUR

DRY

EXPENSIVE

FLIGHT

FLOOD

FOG

FROZEN

HAIL

HAZARDOUS

HEAT

HOLIDAY

ICE

MAP

PLAN

RADAR

RAIN

ROUTE

SEASONAL

SLEET

SLIPPERY

SLUSHY

SMOOTH

SNOW

SPEED

STORM

TIME

WARNINGS

WET

WIND

```
A H U E M I T A E H F A E W
F D E R U S O L C T L C U S
Q R V V O N U Q T O I C S U
F A C I I Z T B F O G I U I
W Z R B S S L E R M H D O U
E Z A O C O N G E S T E D S
T I M O C W R E S L F N R N
U L M K V E O Y P L S T A J
O B E E S W H N O X U S Z P
R D D D L A N O S A E S A T
A E E Y I R D P L D G M H F
D T E L P N W L V I W A R Y
A O P N P I Y A L E D O M J
R U S I E N D N I W Z A R N
Y R D A R G D R A E L C Y C
V N O R Y S U W N M R O T S
```

Solution on Page 313

APPLE	MORNING
BAGEL	NACHOS
BANANA	NUTS
BROWNIES	OLIVES
CAKE	ORANGE
CANDY	PASTRIES
CARROTS	PICKLES
CELERY	POPCORN
CEREAL	PRETZELS
CHEESE	RAISINS
CHIPS	ROLLS
COOKIES	SCONE
CRACKERS	SEEDS
DAILY	SPICY
DIP	SPREADS
FRUIT	TASTY
FUDGE	TOAST
GRANOLA	TREAT
HEALTHY	
JERKY	
KIDS	
LICORICE	

```
V X H K P I C R O L L S T Y
L E G A B A S E N U T S V R
Y S Z U P P S A L O N A R G
T K E R E P C T R E A T S P
E N R L R K L R R L R P E R
S E R E K C A E A I I Y I E
V P A O J C O C F C E H N T
T D I P C O I O Y O K S W Z
S F S H R P P P K R D E O E
A U I A C M O R N I N G R L
O D N D T Z J P K C E L B S
T G S A Y H T L A E H S A E
E E S I C A N D Y R Z E N V
F T G L C H E E S E G E A I
Y T U Y S C O N E A E D N L
T I U R F A M S C L Y S A O
```

Solution on Page 313

BELL

BICYCLE

BMX

BRAKE

CHAIN

CLIMB

COAST

COMMUTE

CRUISE

FAST

FITNESS

FLAT

FRAME

FUN

GEAR

GLOVES

HELMET

LIGHTS

PATH

PEDAL

PUMP

RACE

RIM

ROAD

SAFETY

SCENERY

SEAT

SHIFT

SHORTS

SKID

SPEED

SPOKE

STEER

SUMMER

TIRE

TOUR

TRAIL

WHEEL

WRECK

ZONE

```
X M P R S W S K N U F A H J
K X U A E H S E O R D Q Y X
Z O N E J E Y U A R I M O Z
T K C E W E T M M T K Y Z X
Q C U R R L E S C M S H M E
S F O P U G F O F H E B L F
C L I M B I A Y O L W R L J
W H M U M S S R M I D A O R
K R L P T U T E N G T K Q K
R F E D F S T N S H T E E S
G B I C Y C L E P T S C S G
O L P T K G V C O S A T T X
C H A I N O H S K R F R G B
Q P T D L E K D E I A A D W
W Q H G E D S A H E T I R E
D G D E E P S S G D L L E B
```

Solution on Page 313

BIG DRIFT

BIG SKY

BITTERROOT

BUTTE

CABIN CREEK

CLARK FORK

CROW AGENCY

DEER LODGE

DILLON

GLASGOW

GREAT FALLS

HARDIN

HAVRE

HELENA

HILL COUNTY

KALISPELL

LAKE COUNTY

LAUREL

LIVINGSTON

MILES CITY

PARK COUNTY

POLSON

QUAKE LAKE

RUBY RIVER

SMITH RIVER

TROUT

WOKAL FIELD

YELLOWSTONE

```
T K D Y L L E P S I L A K M
Q E N O T S W O L L E Y L Y
H G B E U N P G H T M A T K
A D I T O K U E O I K N N S
V O G T R E L O L E U W O G
R L D U T E R E C O Y O S I
E R R B N R S O C K Y G L B
V E I A E C U L A C R S O E
I E F T I N L O N D P A P K
R D T T T I L E R U A L P A
Y I Y Y H B G A K T Y G H L
B L S L L A F T A E R G A E
U L Y B W C L A R K F O R K
R O W O K A L F I E L D D A
E N R E V I R H T I M S I U
V C M L I V I N G S T O N Q
```

Solution on Page 313

ANCHOR

BATH

BED

BOW

BUNKS

CABIN

CAPTAIN

CHAIR

CREW

DECK

DOCK

DRIFT

EAT

ESCAPE

EXPLORE

FISH

GALLEY

HOME

LAKE

LIVE

LUXURY

MARINA

MOBILE

MOORED

MOTOR

PORT

RENT

RETIRE

RIVER

ROOMS

ROPE

SAIL

SHORE

SINK

SLEEP

STERN

TRAVEL

WATER

WAVES

YACHT

```
D S W A T E R U E M Y Q T T
M X V P A H D O C K S I N K
E N O T N S C N O U A E X J
Z M A U P I U A R M R L T B
H P O B B F F N Y E S L M K
Q S F H X O N A V K T E G M
G V A G T A W I N V C S B O
L V N E N A R U B I Y E E O
U M R C V I B Y C A R S D R
X Q H E A T A H E S C A P E
U O S R R F A T X L M I M D
R O T O M I C X P P L L M I
Y O P H R R T Z L A E A R E
E E W S E D Z E O H C E G B
N W B W P O R T R A V E L K
K U Z M O B I L E V I L Y S
```

Solution on Page 314

APPALACHIANS

AQUARIA

ART GALLERIES

BEAUTY

BRIDGES

CHINATOWN

DESTINATION

EMPIRE MALL

EVERGLADES

GRAND CANYON

HISTORICAL

LANDMARKS

LEGOLAND

NATIONAL PARK

NIAGARA FALLS

OLD TOWN

PLACES

SALTON SEA

SIGNIFICANCE

SKYSCRAPERS

THEME PARKS

TIMES SQUARE

WAIKIKI BEACH

YELLOWSTONE

ZOOS

```
S R E P A R C S Y K S O O Z
N O Y N A C D N A R G F X Z
O W A I K I K I B E A C H Z
I I M A S K R A P E M E H T
T E N G E M P I R E M A L L
A N L A N D M A R K S P T S
N O A R T Y T U A E B P I E
I T C A A I R A U Q A A M D
T S I F N W O T D L O L E A
S W R A A E S N O T L A S L
E O O L E G O L A N D C S G
D L T L T S E C A L P H Q R
G L S S E G D I R B P I U E
S E I R E L L A G T R A A V
H Y H C H I N A T O W N R E
E C N A C I F I N G I S E K
```

Solution on Page 314

ACCESSORIES	PARTS
BATHROOM	PUMPS
BEVERAGES	REPAIRS
BREAK	REST
CANDY	RIGS
CHIPS	ROADSIDE
COFFEE	SCALE
CONVENIENCE	SEMI
DELI	SNACK
DIESEL	SODA
DINER	SOUVENIRS
DRINKS	STORE
EXIT	STRETCH
FOOD	SUNGLASSES
FUEL	TOYS
GUM	TRAVEL
HAT	TRINKETS
HONK	TRUCKERS
ICE	
JERKY	
MAPS	
OIL	

```
F J P A D Y G V K B S E M I
M E S O S R I N E V U O S Q
D S D E L I O V S T O R E N
Q G R I I H E S B R E A K F
P I F I S R O C H I P S G L
X R E R A D O T C O F F E E
F M U G A P A S P A M C S S
M W E Y F B E O S T N K U E
K S S K C F Y R R E N E N I
J C H R U A E I I I C K G D
U A R E E N N N R I T C L S
T L L J I K E D K S T R A P
O E P D E V C X Y C I O S M
S Y O T N G J U I Y A L S U
C O S O L E V A R T S N E P
F K C R E S T R E T C H S D
```

Solution on Page 314

ABBEY STREET

AER LINGUS

ANNA LIVIA

ASHTOWN CASTLE

BOOK OF KELLS

DARNDALE

DUBLIN CASTLE

GRAFTON STREET

GREENHILLS

HAWKINS STREET

HENRY STREET

HERBERT PARK

JAMES JOYCE

JERVIS STREET

LUAS

MATT TALBOT

MEMORIAL ROAD

RINGSEND

RIVER PODDLE

THE GPO

TONLEGEE ROAD

ULSTER BANK

WORKING CLASS

Solution on Page 314

```
T T E E R T S Y E B B A M O
T O N L E G E E R O A D A M
T K U D M R C E S O S W S E
E K L D A I Y L U K H A L M
E T S O T N O A G O T N L O
R E T P T G J D N F O N I R
T E E R T S S N I K W A H I
S R R E A E E R L E N L N A
Y T B V L N M A R L C I E L
R S A I B D A D E L A V E R
N S N R O H J B A S S I R O
E I K M T H E G P O T A G A
H V E L T S A C N I L B U D
G R A F T O N S T R E E T L
I E W O R K I N G C L A S S
L J H E R B E R T P A R K O
```

Solution on Page 314

BLOUSE

BOOTS

CARDIGAN

CHINOS

COAT

COTTON

DRESS

FLEECE

FOLDABLE

HAT

JACKET

JEANS

LAYERS

LINEN

LOAFERS

LUGGAGE

PACK

PAJAMAS

PANTS

POCKETS

POLO

PONCHO

SANDALS

SCARF

SHIRTS

SHOES

SKIRT

SLACKS

SLEEPWEAR

SNEAKERS

SOCKS

SUIT

SWIMMING

TANK

TIE

TOPS

TRUNKS

UNDERWEAR

WARM

WRINKLED

```
E I T L O L F S M W S V V A
S N E U V P S W R F L S F J
T S K G F A B I A H A L E S
E R C G M C N M W I D A S E
K E A A T K R M P O N C H O
C Y J G L Z M I S S A K I H
O A U E C H I N O S S S R S
P L D N V G E G F C L T T K
A F O L D A B L E A E O S I
N C M A K E E N N R E O S R
T P O E F E R E V D P B E T
S O R T C E N W H I W S R A
C S W E T I R B E G E K D O
A U Z B L O U S E A A C L C
R I R T R U N K S N R O T X
F T A N K E H A T O P S F S
```

Solution on Page 315

BEACH	PICNIC
BIKINI	RECLINE
BLANKET	RELAX
BREEZE	RETREAT
COAST	SALT
COOLER	SAND
CRAB	SEAFOOD
DIVE	SHELLS
DOCK	SNORKEL
DRINKS	SOAK
FIRE	SUN
FLOAT	SWIM
FRISBEE	TAN
FUN	TIDE
HAT	TOWEL
HOT	UNWIND
ISLAND	WATER
LOUNGE	WAVES
OCEAN	
PAIL	
PALM	
PETS	

```
C M G Q B L A N K E T O O U
D J P E S O A K L E W O T K
B G T U W E T E T B B A W T
Y V D K C O D A N S P C R T
H O T O K R B O E I A A L X
E J W A I U R W O R L O I A
C D O H H C A E B F T C C L
W X I U L V D R T I A E E E
E B S T E P E N S A K E R R
M U B S L E I L I T W I S S
N P A H Z G A C C W B K N W
I L A E F N G P N O N A O I
T W V L D U R A D I O U R M
N I O L M O F I R E C L K C
D A Y S K L U D N A S V E T
T U T O F U N H N V I U L R
```

Solution on Page 315

ACADIA

AMERICAN SAMOA

BIG BEND

BISCAYNE

BRYCE CANYON

CANYONLANDS

CAPITOL REEF

CONGAREE

DEATH VALLEY

DENALI

DRY TORTUGAS

GLACIER

GRAND CANYON

GREAT BASIN

KATMAI

KENAI FJORDS

KINGS CANYON

KOBUK VALLEY

MAMMOTH CAVE

MESA VERDE

MOUNT RAINIER

OLYMPIC

SEQUOIA

YOSEMITE

ZION

```
A N S D N A L N O Y N A C Q
K O B U K V A L L E Y H D Y
Q Y M A I D A C A G N E K Q
E N Y A C S I B L O A I A Y
D A I O S K B A Y T N E R S
F C Q N B N C N H G V E A D
S E Q U O I A V S A I G N R
R C E I E C A C C N U E I O
E Y Z R D L A H I T D E S J
E R O N L N T A R R N T A F
R B A E Y O R O E K E I B I
A R Y O M T T V K A B M T A
G A N M N Y A I R T G E A N
N C A U R S F V P M I S E E
O M O D E N A L I A B O R K
C M S M O L Y M P I C Y G P
```

Solution on Page 315

AIRLINE

AIRPORT

ANCESTRY

ARRIVE

BAY

BORDER

BUSINESS

CHECKS

COUNTRY

CRUISE

CUISINE

CULTURE

CURRENCY

CUSTOMS

DEPART

DISCOVER

EXCHANGE

EXPLORE

FAMILY

FLIGHT

FOREIGN

HARBOR

HISTORY

HOTEL

ISLAND

LANDMARK

LANGUAGE

LAYOVER

LEARN

MONUMENT

MUSEUM

OCEAN

RAIL

SAIL

SHIP

STATION

TICKET

TOUR

TROPICS

VISA

```
R T R A P E D N T E B E C T
E Y L L I A S R R H B R O H
D L A M H R O O I A M U U O
R I N C S P L S Y U E T N T
O M G C R P T I S P W L T E
B A U I X O O E N Y E U R L
R F A E R C U R R E N C Y A
A S G Y E M R T H G I L F Y
H C E A V S S E N I S U B O
N I N X O E C A R R I V E V
O P A X C U J J C R U I S E
I O B N S H N T E K C I T R
T R A T I L A N D M A R K A
A T O Y D M O N U M E N T I
T M D N A L S I G V I S A L
S K C E H C F O R E I G N P
```

Solution on Page 315

ALTERNATE

ASPHALT

BARRELS

BLACKTOP

BRIDGE

CAUTION

CEMENT

CLOSURES

CONES

COSTLY

CREW

DAYS

DELAYS

DETOUR

DRAINAGE

ENGINEER

FIX

LANE

LIGHT

MACHINES

MEDIAN

MONTHS

OVERPASS

PAINT

PAVEMENT

POTHOLE

PROJECT

RAMP

ROADS

ROLLER

SAFETY

SHOULDER

SHOVELS

SIGN

SLOW

STOPS

TAR

TRUCKS

WEEKS

WORKERS

```
P U T N E M E C W P T C A S
M M C S N C Y I R A C L L A
A E E D A O W U R V T X I F
R D J A L S O O E E S S G E
K I O O B T L N R M S A H T
B A R R E L S N T E A S T Y
S N P D E Y A N Z N P P R J
L H W R C T I C B T R H U E
E S O U E A B C K P E A C N
V T R U P Z U E O T V L K G
O O K D L N G T S N O T S I
H P E C G D H K I S E P U N
S S R I I O E F U O G S E E
K E S R L E D R A I N A G E
W A B E W S E N I H C A M R
M O N T H S Y A L E D A Y S
```

Solution on Page 316

ACCOUNT	PICTURES
ADVENTURES	PLANS
AGENDA	POSTCARDS
CHRONICLE	RECORD
CULTURE	REMINDERS
DATE	RESEARCH
DESCRIBE	ROUTE
DIARY	SAFARI
DISCOVERY	STOP
DOCUMENT	STUDY
EVENT	THOUGHTS
EXPERIENCE	TOUR
FIELD	TRIP
FOOD	VACATION
HOTELS	VIEWS
ITINERARY	WILDLIFE
LESSONS	WRITE
LOG	
MEMORIES	
NARRATE	
NOTES	
PEOPLE	

```
N O T E S L E T O H F O O D
Q G O L E S S O N S N A L P
W I L D L I F E R U T L U C
P E O P L E N O I T A C A V
A D H C R A E S E R N U A X
S Y R A R E N I T I O E D T
N D R E M I N D E R S M V K
T A R E C N E I R E P X E E
D O R A V S T O P E Y L N M
O A U R C O A I V I C Y T S
C F T R A T C D R I R O U T
U F I E A T S S N A E T R U
M B R O U T E O I E F W E D
E T I R W B R D P D G A S Y
N N E S T H G U O H T A S F
T S A C C O U N T F I E L D
```

Solution on Page 316

AERIAL	NORTH
ATLAS	OBJECT
CITIES	OCEAN
COLORING	PAPER
COMPASS	PLAINS
COUNTRY	RIVER
DESIGN	ROADS
DIRECTION	SCALE
DISTANCE	SEA
DRAWING	SOUTH
EAST	SPATIAL
ELEVATION	STUDY
EXPLORERS	SURVEY
GENERAL	SYMBOLS
GEOGRAPHY	TERRAIN
GPS	TRAVEL
LAND	WEST
LATITUDE	WORLD
LEGEND	
MOUNTAINS	
NAUTICAL	
NAVIGATION	

```
N C G N I W A R D G P S O O
A O N E N I D D E S I G N R
U U I G C N C N I A R R E T
T N R T A N E O L S Y P H R
I T O L A R A I M H A S H A
C R L R A G D T P P C C T V
A Y O L T I I A S A A L U E
L E C A R H R V L I A S O L
T T S I D G E E A S D E S U
D C V G O S C L A N A I P Y
L E G E N D T E A S T T A E
R J G L A T I T U D E I T V
O B S R E R O L P X E C I R
W O M M O U N T A I N S A U
U W P L A I N S Y M B O L S
Y D U T S N A E C O W E S T
```

Solution on Page 316

AIR

ALIGNMENT

BEAD

BELTS

BOLTS

CAR

COOPER

CORDS

DUNLOP

FALKEN

FEDERAL

FLAT

GOODYEAR

GROOVES

HANKOOK

LUG

MAXXIS

MICHELIN

MOUNTING

NITTO

PIRELLI

PLY

PRESSURE

PUMP

RACING

RIM

ROTATION

RUBBER

SHOULDER

SIDEWALL

SNOW

SPARE

TOYO

TREAD

TRUCK

VALVE

WEAR

WHEEL

WINTER

YOKOHAMA

```
F S A G D S M Q L D F X B M
G P S L U G N I C A R A E W
K A I A M A H O K O Y X N I
C R X R R G N I T N U O M N
D E X E E R G A T G R I M T
M W A D P L T O R B C T N E
D H M E O I L O O H E A I R
U E V F O A O I E D I L T U
N E H N C V P L Y R Y F T S
L L A W E D I S M X R E O S
O R N S T N E M N G I L A E
P U K N T X S H O U L D E R
Z B O O B L T D A E R T V P
G B O W E R O T R U C K L U
N E K L A F Y B H O D M A M
J R B C D Q O W K X C J V P
```

Solution on Page 316

ALEXANDRIA

ARABI

BAKER

BATON ROUGE

BELLE CHASSE

BOGALUSA

CHALMETTE

COASTAL

CREOLE

DELTAS

DESTREHAN

FRENCH

GARDERE

GONZALES

HORNETS

IBIS

LAFAYETTE

LAKE CHARLES

LAPLACE

MARSH

METAIRIE

MONROE

NEW ORLEANS

PADDLEFISH

PARISHES

SEDIMENT

SLIDELL

STURGEON

SWAMP

TERRYTOWN

TREE FROGS

WET SAVANNAS

Louisiana

```
E T T E Y A F A L H W L U M
R V E I L A P L A C E L T A
E A L R A R A B I N T E N R
D D O I V E D L R E S D E S
R E E A P G D A D R A I M H
A L R T S U L T N F V L I O
G T C E G O E S A A A S D R
S A H M O R F A X K N N E N
T S A O R N I O E I N A S E
U U L N F O S C L B A E E T
R L M R E T H A A I S L L S
G A E O E A S E H S I R A P
E G T E R B A K E R A O Z M
O O T L T E R R Y T O W N A
N B E L L E C H A S S E O W
C S G D E S T R E H A N G S
```

Solution on Page 317

BARREL

BUBBLE

CANYON

CASCADE

CAVE

CLIFF

DIVE

DROP

EROSION

EXOTIC

FLOWING

GORGE

GUSHING

IMPACT

KAYAKING

LOUD

MISTS

MOUNTAIN

NATURE

NOISY

PLUNGE

POOL

RAFT

RAINBOW

RAPID

RIVER

ROARING

ROCK

RUSH

SCENIC

SHELF

SHOWER

SPLASH

SPRAY

STEEP

STREAM

SWIM

TIER

TOUR

TRICKLE

```
T I E R Z P V R J M I W S U
F T K C O R U G F C L P A I
A A F O D S E N L E S K M P
R E L R H X I I R P R P L E
E Z O O O N F R R F A U E E
V P W T O F A A T C N G R T
I E I Y D B Y O T G N U U S
R C N O I S O R E I Y W T C
I A G I E V I D H S O S A S
C A V E A C Y S I B I S N H
I E M E K T U O N M C R S E
N M A L G G N I K A Y A K L
E K E B T R A U D U L P C F
C S R B O R O E O P O I U O
S Q T U U H N G S M U D R V
P N S B R V X V D Y D V Y M
```

Solution on Page 317

BROCHURE

BUS

CITY

CULTURE

CURRENT

DESCRIBE

DIRECT

EDUCATE

ESCORT

EXPERT

FOOD

FUN

GROUP

HERITAGE

LEAD

LEGENDS

LOCAL

LORE

MEANING

MUSEUM

NATIVE

NICE

PEOPLE

PLANS

POINT

RUINS

SAFARI

SAFETY

SAVVY

SCENERY

SHARE

SIGHTS

SMART

SPEECH

STOP

TALK

TIME

TOURS

TRIP

WALK

```
T R A M S T I E R A H S X E
A S Z U D F P T O U R S D S
L I L G N I N A E M I U B R
K G O V E V I T A N C N U L
H H C M G M F I R A F A S H
E T A U E B U D T R E P X E
R S L T L T N E R R U C J H
I C N N R T E S S N A L P D
T E M I D R U C N U K L A W
A N P O C K D R P H M E X X
G E L P O E P I E C L S Z G
E R U H C O R B R E D C S A
M Y T E F A S E C E R O L X
I S T O P G R O U P C R O E
T U Z I E Y V V A S G T A F
Q U Y R C V D L L Q G T H J
```

Solution on Page 317

ARUBA	PALMS
BEACH	PAPAYA
BREEZY	PLANE
CANOPY	READ
COCONUT	RELAX
DANCE	RESORT
DINING	SAND
DIVING	SCUBA
DRINKS	SEA
FUN	SHOP
GOLF	SPA
HAWAII	SUN
HEAT	SWIM
HIKING	TAN
HOTEL	TOUR
ISLAND	TRAVEL
JUICE	WARM
LOUNGE	WATER
LUAU	
NATURE	
OCEAN	
PACK	

```
C R Q G H V U A U L M E A Q
S X T O U R M R A W R Y H A
H M M L M H U U C U A I P J
O O O F O N K B T P K S A J
P X C T B U Y A A I C L Y R
L L E T V K N P N Z A A Z I
G L A W B V F G O Q P N E L
P E N N W H N N E N N D E T
H J R G E I I I A W A H R T
D I U T V T U N O C O C B F
S K N I R D M I W S D N U S
E P D X C O H D H H H K N W E
S E A A P E S A S C U B A C
D O N L U A L E V A R T T S
C K C E M R I R R E O E E Z
P A E R W S B A N B U D R I
```

Solution on Page 317

AROMATIC

BEANS

BLACK

BLEND

CAFFEINE

CINNAMON

CREAM

CUP

DRINK

FILTER

FLAVOR

FRESH

FRIENDS

FROTHY

GOURMET

GRINDER

GROUND

HOT

ICED

INSTANT

JAVA

JOE

LID

MACHINE

MILD

MOCHA

MORNING

MUG

POT

REGULAR

SAUCER

SIP

SLEEVE

STRONG

SUGAR

SWALLOW

TASTY

VANILLA

WATER

```
A M Z K Z N X Y Q B L A C K
B K U V P U C A F F E I N E
I A S G O U R M E T N Z G V
L R V W M O R E D N I R G E
I V Z A M I F L A V O R M E
M F E A J P I M O C H A W L
S R T Z I D O T A K Y A Y S
C I G N I N R O M C T L H S
C E P Z F S S P S E H L B A
X N U R T N W T R U F I Z U
J D E R F A D A A I G N N C
M S O D N E L B L N W A Y E
H N I Z C B O T U L T V R R
G T M I L D E J G R O U N D
B P K N I R D I E J H W E B
T A S T Y H T O R F M T G D
```

Solution on Page 318

BATH

CLEANSE

CLUB

CURATIVE

ENERGETIC

ENJOY

EXFOLIATE

FACIAL

GUEST

GYM

HEAT

HERBAL

LODGE

LOTION

MANICURE

MASSAGE

MEALS

MINERALS

MUD

NATURAL

OIL

ORGANIC

PAMPER

PEACE

PEDICURE

RECOVER

RELAX

REST

SALTS

SAUNA

SERENITY

SHIATSU

SKIN

STEAM

TABLE

THERAPY

TRANQUIL

WEIGHT

WRAP

YOGA

```
C X H S A W R A P Y M U M L
B A T H K E G D O L M E A E
U L W W S I Z J M A A I X P
L E E T E S N A E L C F T E
C R I L H E N T S A O U S D
A E G A B I S L F L S B E I
Z C H R C A E V I T A R U C
E O T U I I T A A O G H G U
N V R T N Y T I N E R E S R
V E A A A E H P P E A C E
A R N N G S S E G A S S A M
W E Q S R Z T H E R A P Y F
D P U T O H S L A R E N I M
X M I L E F L O T I O N U Y
D A L A B R E H Q L I D E G
A P T S A U N A G O Y Y N K
```

Solution on Page 318

BED

BIG

BLISSFUL

BUTLER

CLASSY

COMFORT

DELUXE

ELEGANT

ELEVATOR

FAMOUS

FANCY

FEATURES

FRILLS

GILDED

GRAND

HARDWOOD

HIGH

HOTEL

JACUZZI

KEY

LUXURY

MAJESTIC

MARBLE

OPULENT

ORNATE

PREMIUM

PRIVATE

REGAL

RELAX

RICH

RITZY

ROOM

SERVICE

SKYLINE

SPA

STYLISH

TERRACE

VIEW

WEALTHY

WELCOME

```
J F A M O U S T Y L I S H F
G I L D E D X A L E R K F O
U Z M H C I R J R H C Y R M
L U X U R Y A O R I D L I A
O Q Y L I C O K T G N I L R
R Y Y E U M H S V H A N L B
N P C Z K F E A T U R E S L
A R Z N T J S R R N G L C E
T I S P A I Z S P D R E O X
E V B M C F R H I E W T M U
U A U R O T A V E L E O F L
I T T S E R V I C E B H O E
W E L C O M E R E G A L R D
T W E I V T E R R A C E T E
U T R C O P U L E N T G I B
I S C L A S S Y H T L A E W
```

Solution on Page 318

BAG	RACE
BIKER	RIDER
BOOTS	ROAD
BRAKE	ROUTE
CHOPPER	SAFETY
CLUB	SEAT
COURSE	SPEED
DRIVE	SPORT
ENGINE	START
FAST	STOP
FUN	STRAP
GAS	STUNTS
GLOVES	TANK
HANDLE	TIRE
HELMET	TOUR
JACKET	VISOR
JUMP	WHEEL
MOPED	WIND
MOTOR	
PARK	
POWER	
QUICK	

```
C W X B G J R J E E B Q Q B
G E V I R D E P O M S T V Y
D S R K C I U Q T K O B S H
J Y T E O J S B V R R D J H
X H W R P T G U R Y O A T A
R W Q M A P L L V A C P P N
W R U O T P O C Q K K R S D
I J R O S I V H E L M E T L
N P J T I R E T C U S W N E
D W G A S D S R M O H O U N
B W H E E L A K O F U P T I
J K A E R C F R A T R R S G
S T P T E U E S B O O T S N
J S U U N D T B A G O M D E
Y L V O I Y Y D R P F Z C Z
S T A R T A N K K R X D V O
```

Solution on Page 318

BAR

BED

BRUNCH

BUDGET

BUFFET

BUSINESS

COMFORT

DESK

ENTRANCE

EXERCISE

FLAMINGO

FOYER

GYM

HILTON

HYATT

LINENS

LODGING

LUGGAGE

LUXOR

MAID

MANAGER

MARRIOTT

MEALS

MIRAGE

MOTEL

PALAZZO

PATRON

PEABODY

POOL

RAMADA

RESORT

ROOM

SAUNA

SPA

SUITE

TOWELS

TRAVEL

UPGRADE

VALET

VIEW

```
E R T S U I T E L A V I E W
M O O R J C R T E F F U B H
P A L A Z Z O D L T O B E D
U R E G A N A M R J Y U Y T
H L E V A R T A F N E D L B
Y U B R G Q B R M O R G O L
A X R P A E U R A R R E O M
T O U R L X S I D T V T P Q
T R N T E E I O A A F E E W
O W C R T R N T M P L G A N
W K H O O C E T A N A A B D
E E S S M I S P R G M R O I
L I N E N S S J G A I I D A
S J A R D E M U C A N M Y M
U L Z N H I L T O N G C Y G
S A U N A G N I G D O L E G
```

Solution on Page 319

ACCENT

ADJECTIVE

AFRIKAANS

ALPHABET

ARABIC

BENGALI

CANTONESE

CONJUGATE

DIALECT

DIALOGUE

ENGLISH

FRENCH

GERMAN

GRAMMAR

HINDI

IMMERSION

ITALIAN

JAPANESE

KOREAN

LATIN

LESSON

LISTEN

MANDARIN

NOUN

PERSIAN

PRACTICE

PUNJABI

RUSSIAN

SIGN

SPANISH

SPEAK

STUDY

TAMIL

TEACHER

TURKISH

TUTOR

URDU

VERB

WRITING

```
N A M R E G N I T I R W F G
S N O U N I R A D N A M R J
N K A E P S M A I Q E T E N
A N O S S E L M M S A C N I
A D J E C T I V E M S Z C T
K B E N G A L I I R A U H A
I K P O P G L L U D S R R L
R V R T V U J P I D N I H I
F S A N E J N A H V R P O A
A P C A R N L J T A E U R N
K A T C B O G C A R B A T E
O N I E G C E L S B B E U T
R I C U D L J I I I I O T S
E S E N A P A J C S C A O I
A H S I G N T E A C H E R L
N Y D U T S H S I K R U T Q
```

Solution on Page 319

AVENUES	PARK PLACE
BROADWAY	PASSERSBY
BUS	PAVEMENT
CAR	POLLUTION
COMMUTE	PROTEST
CONCRETE	RETAILERS
CORNERS	SEWER
DIRECTIONS	SIGN
DISTRICT	SMELL
DIVERSITY	STOP
ENCOUNTERS	SUBWAY
ENERGY	TAXIS
EXPLORE	TOURIST
HOUSES	TRAFFIC
HUB	TRAVEL
JOURNEY	TREES
LIFE	URBAN
LITTER	WALK
MAIN	
MARKET	
MOVEMENT	
OFFICES	

```
M T N E M E V O M A R K E T
D C L E V A R T H O U S E S
L I T T E R H U B M A I N I
W R V O P A V E M E N T K R
A T P E A E A V E N U E S U
L S R S R E T N U O C N E O
K I O T K S W E O S O E W T
Y D T O P E I F R I I R E E
E B E P L F F T T C A G R X
N I S H A I L C Y C N Y N P
R T T R C L E T U M M O C L
U A S E E R T R A F F I C O
O X S M I S R E L I A T E R
J I S D U A S R E N R O C E
U S U B W A Y A W D A O R B
N O I T U L L O P N A B R U
```

Solution on Page 319

BANKING

BEACHES

BELLEFONTE

BLADES

BRIDGEVILLE

CAMDEN

CHESWOLD

CLAYTON

COLONIAL

DELAWARE CITY

DELMAR

DOVER

ELSMERE

FELTON

GEORGETOWN

HARRINGTON

KENT

LENAPE

MIDDLETOWN

MILLSBORO

NANTICOKE

NEW CASTLE

NEWARK

NEWPORT

OCEAN VIEW

RIVERFEST

SELBYVILLE

THE WEDGE

TOWNSEND

WYOMING

ZWAANENDAEL

```
B S J T N W O T E L D D I M
A P N F F O C E A N V I E W
N E W C A S T L E E L L K W
K W Y O M I N G Y L O Y O E
I U C L A Y T O N L T O C G
N E L L I V E G D I R B I D
G W S E D A L B C V R E T E
C R O R A M L E D Y C R N W
H I R T N D R L T B O E A E
E V O B E A N L O L L M N H
S E B E W G K E W E O S O T
W R S A P R R F N S N L T L
O F L C O E A O S A I E L W
L E L H R V W N E P A N E L
D S I E T O E T N G L W F U
B T M S W D N E D M A C Z J
```

Solution on Page 319

AIR BAG

ALERT

ATTENTION

BELT

BLIND SPOT

BOTH HANDS

BRAKE

CAREFULLY

CAUTION

CELL PHONE

COURTESY

DEFENSIVE

DISTANCE

FOCUS

GUARDED

HORN

LAW

LICENSE

LIGHTS

LOOK

MAINTENANCE

MARKERS

MIRRORS

OBSERVE

OIL

PARK

PATIENT

PEDESTRIAN

REPAIRS

RULES

SIGNS

SLOW

SPEED

STEER

STOP

TIRES

TRAFFIC

WARNINGS

WATCH

YIELD

```
T S R I A P E R W A L E R T
I R E E T S A W A T C H U G
R O M D N C L A S N G I S A
E R C E D E D R A U G F H B
S R C F B L I N D S P O T R
O I D E D L E I Y D R C T I
L M I N E T S N E N P U N A
T E S S N C P G V A T S E T
R E T I O A E S R H M N I T
A C A V H R E K E H A O T E
F M N E P E D E S T R I A N
F K C K L F B L B O K T P T
I O E A L U K E O B E U O I
C O O R E L S E L U R A T O
O L I B C L I G H T S C S N
W O L S A Y S E T R U O C B
```

Solution on Page 320

ADOBE

ARCHITECT

ART DECO

BEAUTIFUL

BRICK

BUILDING

CHURCH

CITIES

CLASSIC

COLONIAL

COLUMN

CREATIVE

DESIGN

DIVERSE

ECLECTIC

ENGLISH

FEDERAL

FRONTIER

GEORGIAN

GLASS

GOTHIC

HISTORY

HOUSES

JEFFERSON

LANDSCAPE

LINES

LOG CABIN

MODERN

MONUMENTS

PLANS

PUEBLO

ROOF

SPANISH

STEEL

VARIETY

WINDOWS

WOOD

```
S P A N I S H I S T O R Y B
L A I N O L O C M O D E R N
N O C H E B B B D O O W I C T
M O G R C P E C L E C T I C
U S S C E R A O R K S N S E
L N T R A A U C C O W O S T
O A G N E B T H S E O R A I
C L E N E F I I C D D F L H
I P O H I M F N V X N T C C
H P R K S D U E L E I A R R
T U G G E I L N J E W C L A
O E I L N V L I O N E I I D
G B A A I E M G U M J T M O
D L N S L R B O N B C I S B
H O U S E S L A R E D E F E
D V A R I E T Y N G I S E D
```

Solution on Page 320

ANCHOR

BAY

BREEZE

CANOE

CAPTAIN

CHOPPY

COOLER

DECK

DIVING

DOLPHINS

FISH

FLOAT

FUN

KAYAK

LAKE

MOTOR

OARS

OCEAN

PADDLES

PUMP

RACE

RELAXING

RIVER

ROCKING

SAIL

SCENIC

SCHOONER

SEA

SKI

SPEED

STEER

TIDE

TOUR

TRAVEL

VEST

VIEW

VOYAGE

WATER

WIND

YACHT

```
S D T R A V E L A W W V N A
L N V E S T H I A W U O M C
N A P L M W S G P K I G S X
D E R O C K I N G N E N F S
R C T O I P F I S E I L D S
H O X C T S S X C H O P P Y
R S P U M P X A P A A M G A
V W E I V E R L T Q R L N J
T G G L K E O E A L S C I Z
I J A A D D Y R N E H A V T
D Q Y R R D G I B O S R I Y
E A O T E D A A R C O E D L
K O V H E T Y P E I H H A E
F U N C P X A N E T V Z C P
K G K A F C I W Z R E E T S
G Z C Y C C B G E T O U R G
```

Solution on Page 320

BONDING

CABIN

CANDLES

CELEBRATE

CHOCOLATE

COUPLE

DANCING

DINNER

ELOPE

ESCAPE

EXCITING

FLIGHT

HOTEL

ISLAND

LOVE

MARRIAGE

MOUNTAIN

MUSIC

OCEAN

PARADISE

PEACEFUL

PICNIC

QUIET

RESORT

ROMANCE

ROSES

SATURDAY

SOLITUDE

SPA

STARS

STROLL

SUNSET

SURPRISE

TALK

TICKETS

TRIP

TROPICAL

VISIT

WALKS

WEEKEND

```
E H E T C G G N I D N O B E
P S P H S T E K C I T W S W
O P A G N I C N A D A I Q E
L A C I P O R T O L R U V E
E S S L C L N T K P I O C K
C R E F H U M S R E L E K E
A A C X O E D U T I L O S N
B T N M C M S L S E P I D D
I S A D O I A A B I D S L V
N T M Y L T T R T A C L U S
A I O L A E A I R U D A F E
E S R L T T S A N I R N E S
C I K O E X P B N G A D C O
O V U R P I C N I C O G A R
C L E T O H E C O U P L E Y
N R E S O R T E S N U S P G
```

Solution on Page 320

ATCHISON

BEAMER BARN

BIG BRUTUS

DICKINSON

DODGE CITY

DONIPHAN

EISENHOWER

EMPORIA

GARDNER

GREAT BEND

HARVEY

HAYS

HUTCHINSON

JOHN BROWN

LIBERAL

MANHATTAN

MCPHERSON

MONTGOMERY

OLATHE

OLD WEST

OSAWATOMIE

OXLEY BARN

OZ MUSEUM

PAUL BOYER

PITTSBURG

RILEY

ROCK CITY

SALINA

SHOCKERS

WYANDOTTE

```
E H T A L O X L E Y B A R N
H A R V E Y T I C E G D O D
N X E T T O D N A Y W N S O
O S A W A T O M I E P E A N
S O O L D W E S T I A B L I
I B I G B R U T U S U T I P
H N L I B E R A L E L A N H
C O G A R D N E R N B E A A
T S R E K C O H S H O R T N
A N M U E S U M Z O Y G T A
D I C K I N S O N W E T A I
H H M O N T G O M E R Y H R
A C Q H J O H N B R O W N O
Y T I C K C O R I L E Y A P
S U Q K N O S R E H P C M M
W H P V P I T T S B U R G E
```

Solution on Page 321

ADVERTISING

AUDI

AUTOMOBILE

BAJA BUG

BEETLE

CABRIOLET

CAMPER

CARS

COMPACT

CONVERTIBLE

COUPE

DASHER

EOS

GERMANY

GOLF

HATCHBACK

HIPPIE VAN

INTERNATIONAL

JETTA

KARMANN GHIA

LEMON

MICROBUS

MINIVAN

PASSAT

RABBIT

ROUTAN

SCIROCCO

SEDAN

THINK SMALL

TIGUAN

WOLFSBURG

WORLDWIDE

```
W C R O U T A N A U G I T D
O W O L F S B U R G Y V A A
R L W N F M N A D E S D N S
L N E Z V J I A O I V O T H
D B K M L E S C V E W E E E
W Y A A O H R C R I L Z R R
I N T E R N A T I O N A L T
D A T E W M I T I R B I L C
E M E D P S A R C B O U M A
L R J E I U B N I H L C S P
T E R N K A O T N M B E C M
E G G R C C T C E G S A W O
E O L L A M S K N I H T C C
B L D R N A V E I P P I H K
V F S E L I B O M O T U A C
H B A J A B U G P A S S A T
```

Solution on Page 321

ALAMO

ASPEN

BEAUTY

BORDERS

CARS

CATTLE

CITIES

CUISINE

DINERS

DRIVE

EAST

FARMS

FIELDS

FLIGHTS

HIGHWAY

HISTORY

LAKE

MOUNTAIN

MUSEUMS

NAPA

NATIONAL

NEW YORK

NORTH

OCEAN

PARKS

ROAD

ROCKIES

RUSHMORE

SCHOOLS

SHOPS

SIGNS

SOUTH

STATES

TOLLS

TOWNS

TRAFFIC

TRAVEL

TRUCKS

VEGAS

WEST

Across the USA

```
X V T R U C K S K R A P Z S
F N S T O T W A M S W K B H
Y L A K E A S G B U R B H O
S Y E B O R D E R S E A E P
R L R K K N U V W A S S C S
E E O O R N A S U T D P U R
N V C O T O C T H A B E I M
I A K S H S Y G I M P N S E
D R I O A C I W V O O A I L
F T E U I L S H E U N R N T
A F S T F E S I G N S A E T
R I I H V T G O O T B Z L A
M E R I A U M T R A F F I C
S L R T Y A W H G I H F D H
O D E T L H T R O N A E C O
L S M A S L L O T O W N S G
```

Solution on Page 321

PUZZLES • 185

BAG

BIRDIE

BUDDIES

CADDY

CART

CLUB

COOLER

COURSE

DRIVER

EAGLE

ENJOY

FAIRWAY

FLAG

FLIGHT

FOCUS

FRIENDS

GREEN

HAT

HILLS

HOLE

IRONS

LEISURE

LINKS

LODGE

PAR

PIN

POND

PRO SHOP

PUTT

RELAX

RESORT

ROUND

SAND

SCORE

TEE

TOWEL

TRAVEL

UNWIND

VIEWS

WEDGE

Golf Trip

```
G D Y D E B V L B J X W C S
E H F S N C A I I O X Q Q V
D E O R L O D G E G D E W B
S N T L I L P S F W V F T M
C J N E E E I R O N S P C L
O O Q V T I N H G P O O T O
R Y U A R S F D X H O C D L
E D N R O U A D S L S A N D
F T E T S R I O E I D R I B
L O E Q E E R R I U T T W U
P W R A R P W C D Y H H N L
N E G E A U A F D R G C U C
G L L M P T Y D U L I N K S
E A I B A T A H B A L V I W
X U L S U C O F G D F D E P
R Y E F C O F S S D N U O R
```

Solution on Page 321

PUZZLES • 187

ACCIDENT

AGENT

AGREEMENT

APPRAISER

BROKER

CARRIER

CLAIM

COLLISION

COMPANY

CONTRACT

COSTLY

CRASH

CREDIT

DRIVERS

ESSENTIAL

EXPENSIVE

FLOOD

LEGAL

LIABILITY

LIMIT

LOSS

MANDATORY

MONTHLY

NECESSARY

NEEDED

PAYMENT

PLAN

PREMIUM

QUOTATION

RATE

RENEW

REPAIRS

REQUIRED

RISK

SAFETY

SECURITY

VANDALISM

```
T W D R I V E R S D O O L F
I T B R O K E R E I R R A C
M Y N Y L T S O C S S O L O
I Y T E F A S I U E T A R M
L S P I M T C A R T N O C P
M G L C L E S P I M E Q U A
O A A Y O I E P T L M U G N
N M N C R L B R Y E Y O M Y
T U E D C A L A G G A T S R
H I E E A I S I I A P A I E
L M D R T T D S S L K T L P
Y E E I I N O E E I H I A A
M R D U D E E R N C O O D I
X P D Q E S Y G Y T E N N R
W E N E R S C L A I M N A S
H S A R C E X P E N S I V E
```

Solution on Page 322

ATHLETIC

BANDEAU

BATHING SUIT

BIKINI

BOXER

BRIEFS

COLORFUL

COVER

DESIGNER

ENHANCING

FITNESS

HALTER

HYBRID

JAMMERS

LINING

MINIMIZING

MODEST

PADDED

RACER

REVEALING

SARONG

SEPARATES

SPANDEX

SPEEDO

STRAPS

TANKINI

THONG

TIES

TIGHT

TRUNKS

UNITARD

WATERPROOF

WETSUIT

WRAP

```
R E V O C R M S P A R T S B
S Z H K D O E G G H X F Q Y
P A D D E D L T T S E D O M
E U I P D J R O L I B Y K E
E A R M S E P A R A T E S S
D E B Z I R V B T F H F S W
O D Y Y H N E H G I U E P A
E N H A N C I N G B N L A T
T A N K I N I M G T O U N E
H B I J G L G T I I N X D R
O V N S A N B F E Z S R E P
N T U E O M I I T L I E X R
G I V R Y P M N K H H N D O
T E A X Q A C E I I G T G O
R S K N U R T G R L N I A F
R A C E R W W E T S U I T N
```

Solution on Page 322

ALTOONA

AMES

ANKENY

BETTENDORF

BURLINGTON

CEDAR FALLS

CEDAR RAPIDS

CLIVE

CORALVILLE

COUNCIL BLUFFS

DALLAS COUNTY

DES MOINES

FORT DODGE

GEODE

HAWKEYE

IOWA CITY

JOHNSON COUNTY

LINN COUNTY

MARION

MARSHALLTOWN

NEWTON

OAK

POLK COUNTY

SCOTT COUNTY

STORY COUNTY

WARREN COUNTY

WILD ROSE

```
Z W D J I O W A C I T Y C Y
T C E O Z X M A M A T O T H
Y E S H H E L A M N U N E A
T D M N S T R E U N U C K W
N A O S O I V O C O M O A K
U R I O O I C I C F A R C E
O F N N L Y L N R G R A E Y
C A E C R B N O A E S L D E
T L S O L I D N N O H V A G
T L T U L N K C K D A I R D
O S F N E E O A B E L L R O
C F Y T N U O C S A L L A D
S F T Y N O T W E N T E P T
D E Y T N U O C K L O P I R
B P Y E S O R D L I W V D O
A B U R L I N G T O N Y S F
```

Solution on Page 322

ANIMALS	MONKEY
ANTS	NATURE
BEAUTY	PADDLE
BOAT	RAPIDS
BUGS	RIVER
CABIN	ROCK
CANOE	SAFARI
COBRA	SHIP
COUGAR	SHORE
DINING	SNAKES
FAUNA	TIGER
FISH	TOUR
FLOAT	TRAVEL
FOOD	TREK
FROGS	VINES
GUIDE	VOYAGE
HIPPOS	WATER
HUMID	ZEBRA
JAGUAR	
LAGOON	
LION	
MACAW	

Jungle Cruise

```
R I V E R N K X T B H T Q T
E B F O V I Q S R E T A W O
G U O I Y B P N W R R T B B
I G W A C A M A E T A O L F
T S A S T C G K D M V U M I
D B A T D W F E G D E R K S
I Z N N W I S S K Y L Y N H
V E U A R F P M O N K E Y H
I B A A R W S A E R U T A N
N R F O D H X G R T U H F C
E A G O I A N I M A L S L O
S S O P P I H O E N G A D B
H F D U N K K B J A G U A R
O G U I D E C A N O E F O A
R H D I M U H O O R D T P C
E R Q N L I O N R U T I W C
```

Solution on Page 322

BAG

BLOUSE

BOOK

BRUSH

CAMERA

CASH

CLOTHES

COMPUTER

CONTACTS

DOCUMENTS

DRESS

GLASSES

HAT

JACKET

LOTIONS

LUGGAGE

MAP

MEDICINE

MONEY

MUSIC

PACK

PANTS

PASSPORT

PILLOW

PLANS

RAZOR

REMEMBER

SCHEDULE

SHIRTS

SHOES

SKIRT

SNACKS

SOAP

SOCKS

SWIMSUIT

TICKETS

TISSUES

TOYS

UMBRELLA

VACCINES

```
S K I R T R A Z O R P M N B
S C H W F U M B R E L L A C
S H A A T I C K E T S G S P
E E I M U S I C B U E T W H
R O O R E B P O M X N O I P
D G W H T R T M E E I Y M A
T R O P S S A P M L C S S O
K E S D H A S U E U I V U S
T S L E M S C T R G D A I O
E N S U U O U E C G E C T C
K A N D D S N R Y A M C E K
C L O T H E S E B G T I S S
A P I J V A H I Y E O N U P
J S T N A P T C T D U E O A
B O O K G L A S S E S S L C
P I L L O W S K C A N S B K
```

AACHEN

AUTOBAHN

BACH

BEER

BERLIN

BIELEFELD

BOCHUM

BONN

BRATWURST

BREMEN

CHEESE

COLOGNE

DEUTSCHE BAHN

DORTMUND

DUISBURG

EINSTEIN

ENGINEERS

ESSEN

FRANKFURT

GYMNASIUM

INVENTORS

LUFTHANSA

MAX PLANCK

MUNICH

MUSIC

NUREMBERG

SAUERKRAUT

SAUSAGES

SAXONY

SPORTS

STUTTGART

TRAINS

WUPPERTAL

```
J L H G K S A U S A G E S T
S Y K Y W U P P E R T A L R
D N U M T R O D E U E C S U
E O I N D R B B O C H U M F
I X L A T L M U S I C I H K
N A G S R E E N I G N E C N
S S T I R T N F W V O N I A
T D E U T S C H E B A H N R
E U N M A J J N A L A R U F
I I G N U R T C P B E C M N
N S O E O O K X H E O I H E
I B L S R B A R B E V T B H
L U O S Q M B R E M E N U C
R R C E B R A T W U R S T A
E G L U F T H A N S A I E A
B P K T R A G T T U T S P S
```

Solution on Page 323

AGILITY

BRAKES

CLUTCH

CORVETTE

COSTLY

DRIVE

ENGINE

EXHAUST

FAST

FERRARI

GAS

GEARS

INTAKE

JAGUAR

MACHINE

MILES

MOTOR

NIMBLE

PISTONS

POPULAR

PORSCHE

POWER

PRICEY

QUICK

RACE

REV

RIDE

ROADWAY

SHIFT

SLEEK

SMOOTH

SPEED

THRILL

THROTTLE

TICKETS

TORQUE

TURBO

UPSCALE

VALUABLE

ZOOM

Speedy Autos

```
Z W V S H I F T U R B O Q T
O S G G C X Y Y E C I R P D
O Q E F T O A L S M A G C E
M J A G U A R P T L A B S E
U S R V L B O V U S E N T P
T E S A C D T P E X O E E S
V Q E L T T O R H T Y C K E
K C I U Q P M A S O T X C L
I N T A K E U I L R I E I I
U I Z B C S P L B Q L N T M
P M E L T O I R D U I I B R
S B F E R R A R I E G H Q E
C L T S H K I R X U A C S W
A E C T E V R O A D W A Y O
L H P S E A R H T O O M S P
E N G I N E C A R I D E J N
```

Solution on Page 323

AIRPORT

AISLE

ALTITUDE

ARRIVAL

BAGS

BOARDING

BOOK

BUSINESS

CLAIM

COST

DELAY

DIVERT

FUN

GATE

HOP

JOURNEY

JUMP

LANDING

LAYOVER

LINES

LUGGAGE

MEAL

MOVIE

MUSIC

PILOT

PLAN

REST

ROUTE

SAFETY

SEAT

SNACK

STEWARD

TARMAC

TICKET

TRAVEL

TRIP

UPDATE

VISA

VOYAGE

WINDOW

```
B L T R E L M C K K J M L Z
L M C L U E I V O M G S F W
E A S A T Z S N A C K W F H
V I Y S R U I T E K C I T J
A V O O S R V S F S I N R U
R C Y G V E I G U G S D E M
T I A F R E N V N X U O V P
N B T R O P R I A I M W I G
A L T I T U D E S L D L D M
L P J O U R N E Y U O N R E
P A X T A U G O T T B V A A
H S R O B A P A E H O P W L
T I B O G P R D F Y A L E D
P V O G U M M I A L C E T X
C K U D A T C G S T A E S X
Q L N C T S E R J Z E T A G
```

Solution on Page 323

BALANCE

BASS

BLUES

BUTTON

CABLES

CHANNEL

CONTROL

COUNTRY

DASH

DETACH

DISC

EJECT

FADE

GOSPEL

INPUT

KNOB

MUSIC

NEWS

OLDIES

OUTPUT

PRESETS

PROGRAM

REMOTE

ROCK

SEARCH

SEEK

SOUND

SPORTS

STEREO

STOCK

SYSTEM

TALK

TRAFFIC

TREBLE

TUNE

TWEETER

VOLUME

WATTS

WEATHER

WOOFER

```
G M U S I C O T U P T U O X
R E F O O W A M V W T Y Z K
A F K B F Z T B E O R U E T
M H C H A N N E L T L E N C
K N O B D L T M N E S U W E
H U T M E E A U Q S S Y M J
E C S A R C O N T R O L S E
K C O R L C I E C W L W B T
L J R G F L S D B E W U B O
A Q Q O T E E A P A T V L M
T D G R R T S S T T D D U E
Y E W P A S O T O H I N E R
D I S C F G S N E E H U S N
R A H W F X Z I S R B O P E
T U P N I T R E B L E S Y W
D A S H C R A E S T R O P S
```

Solution on Page 324

ALOE	PIER
BALL	PLAY
BLANKET	RADIO
BOOK	SAND
CLAM	SEAWEED
CLOTHING	SHELLS
COOLER	SHOVEL
CRABS	SNACKS
DUNE	SNORKEL
FINS	SURF
FISH	SWIM
FLIPPERS	TAN
FRISBEE	TIDE
GLASSES	TOWEL
GOGGLES	VISOR
HAT	WALK
LOTION	WATER
MAGAZINE	WAVES
OCEAN	
OYSTER	
PAIL	
PICNIC	

Going to the Beach

```
R K S C K K M A G A Z I N E
S Y L O T I O N I T S J H C
P A O A K R I P A I L S Y Q
M B C J W H O O F D L K A G
P B O L T E A S R E E C L Q
I B O O H X G T I B H A P E
L F L I P P E R S V S N L R
D C E A I I D L B S X S E L
N U R C N A B E E S S T E O
A H N A C K Z S E V A W I O
S I S E B X E L N W O D I P
C G F I N S G T N O A H I M
V A T A F G L R A R R E S G
V P T R O Y S T E R R K S H
M C U G W K G I C T O W E L
L S L B K F A L O E B A L L
```

Solution on Page 324

PUZZLES • 207

BRITISH MUSEUM

DAHESH

EGYPTIAN

ENCYCLOPEDIC

FIELD MUSEUM

GOLD MUSEUM

GRAND PALAIS

HISTORIC

IMAX

ISRAEL MUSEUM

LACMA

LOUVRE

MACBA

MODERN

MUSEO SOUMAYA

MUSEU PICASSO

MUSEUM OF ART

PALAZZO DUCALE

PERGAMON MUSEUM

PLANETARIA

PRADO

RUSSIAN MUSEUM

SCIENCE

THE MET

UFFIZI GALLERY

```
P Y G O L D M U S E U M M Z
P E R V U O L O C G H U U P
M R R E E X A M I Y I E S A
U U E G L V C Z E P S S E Y
E S E N A L M I N T T U U A
S S G S C M A T C I O M M M
U I R P U Y O G E A R D O U
M A A L D M C N I N I L F O
L N N A O T H L M Z C E A S
E M D N Z E S S O U I I R O
A U P E Z M E M I P S F T E
R S A T A E H A O T E E F S
S E L A L H A C D D I D U U
I U A R A T D B C H E R I M
Z M I I P O D A R P K R B C
O S S A C I P U E S U M N J
```

Solution on Page 324

ABERDEEN

ANNAPOLIS

ANTIETAM CREEK

BARREN ISLAND

BOWIE

BROOMES ISLAND

CANALS

CECIL COUNTY

COBB ISLAND

DELAWARE RIVER

GARRETT ISLAND

GIBSON ISLAND

GLEN BURNIE

GREENBELT

HARFORD COUNTY

HOWARD COUNTY

LAUREL

MANOKIN RIVER

MILLER ISLAND

ORIOLES

PORT

ROCKVILLE

TAKOMA PARK

Solution on Page 324

```
R E V I R N I K O N A M T D
C E C I L C O U N T Y G M H
D Y V B G R E E N B E L T D
A N T I E T A M C R E E K N
Y C A N R S I L O P A N N A
T O K L U E I W O B L B E L
N B O C S O R C R Z A U E S
U B M A S I C A O P U R D I
O I A N P Y S D W N R N R N
C S P A L D B E R A E I E O
D L A L T R O P M O L E B S
R A R S E L O I R O F E A B
A N K E L L I V K C O R D I
W D N A L S I T T E R R A G
O D N A L S I N E R R A B H
H D N A L S I R E L L I M A
```

Solution on Page 324

ANCHOR

BAIT

BARGE

BEACH

BOBBERS

BREEZE

BUOY

CANOE

CRANE

CREW

DECK

DOCK

FISHERMAN

HOOKS

HORIZON

HULL

INLET

JETTY

KAYAK

KNOT

LAGOON

MARINA

MAST

MOTOR

OAR

OCEAN

OTTERS

PEOPLE

PIER

PORT

ROPE

SAIL

SEAGULLS

SEAWEED

SHIP

STERN

TIE

WATER

WAVES

WINDY

```
Q B M S J E T T Y B Z P H Q
Y D N I W O X L K I E M O M
X F K A W N N A N I R A M G
R E I R E A N L Q R S S C D
W G N S E C E S S H E T L H
K N B P H T O Z L O V T S E
B G O O S E A Z L R A O S D
B R R O B T R W U I W N X V
T R E T G B K M G Z P K J X
P D E E W A E S A O K C E D
I E P I Z R L R E N A C H M
E G O T T E R S S N Y O U B
R R R P I H K C K S A I L J
N A A I L A R C W O K R L H
X B O H B E B R O T O M C V
Y R A S W W H O X D A H Z K
```

Solution on Page 325

BRAKES

CAB

CONTENTS

DELIVERY

DIESEL

DINER

DISTANCE

ENGINE

FREIGHT

FUEL

GOODS

HANDLE

HAUL

HEAVY

HIGHWAY

HOURS

JOB

LAWS

LIGHTS

LOAD

MAP

MEAL

MOTEL

MUSIC

OPERATOR

PALLET

RADIO

REST

RIG

ROAD

ROUTE

SCHEDULE

SEMI

SERVICE

SHIPPER

STOP

TRACTOR

TRAILER

WEIGHT

WHEELS

```
L E U F C S D O O G V K M T
U T I M E S T H G I E W N W
A U B K L E G Y B T S E R S
H O A E L Y D I S T A N C E
J R E L I A R T N D A O R R
B H A J S C H E D U L E H V
W P G L O E T K V H N U X I
R B Q R A N T H G I E R F C
S J A V O W B N D G L R G E
K M Y C O T S O I H D E T N
G O S O I D A R E W N P D G
S T R A C T O R S A A P C I
A E U L S Z S O E Y H I U N
P L O S T H G I L P S H K E
X A H L O K L J L U O S I X
D Z M B P G Q H M E A L U E
```

Solution on Page 325

AERIAL

ALTITUDE

CONTINENT

CONTOURS

CRATER

DETAILS

DRAINAGE

EARTH

ELEVATION

FEATURES

FORESTS

GEOGRAPHY

GRADIENT

HEIGHT

HILLS

KEY

LANDFORM

LATITUDE

LEGEND

LINES

MAP

MESA

MILE

NATION

PARKS

PLACE

RELIEF

REMOTE

RIVERS

SCALE

SCIENCE

SEA

SHAPE

SLOPE

STATE

SURFACE

SURVEY

TERRAIN

VALLEY

WATER

```
S N O I T A N L E G E N D Z
H T R A E S A R E M O T E S
A S E P R I E L A C S K X T
P L O E R T S C I E N C E M
E L V E A G E O G R A P H Y
S I A R I S T N E I D A R G
R H C C N O I T A V E L E V
D W L S E H E I G H T D I A
E C A U R G M N C W U P S L
T R N R E U A E D T A E T L
A E D V L C O N I M M T S E
I L F E I L A T I T U D E Y
L I O Y M T L F N A R V R R
S E R U T A E F R O R J O G
D F M P A R K S Z U C D F C
S T A T E R L I N E S E A E
```

Solution on Page 325

AFRICA

AMAZON

ANCIENT

ANIMALS

ARUBA

BAHAMAS

BALI

BEACH

BEIJING

BRAZIL

CLIMATE

CULTURE

CURIOUS

DESERT

DUBAI

ECUADOR

EGYPT

EXPLORE

FIJI

FOREIGN

HAWAII

HONDURAS

INDIA

ISLAND

JUNGLE

MALDIVES

MOROCCO

NEW

PARIS

PERU

PLANTS

ROMANTIC

SAHARA

SCENIC

TAHITI

TOUR

TRAVEL

UNIQUE

UNUSUAL

VENICE

```
A D N A L S I R A P A B D C
B I A M A Z O N T R R U I H
U N I Q U E V L A A E N A E
R D T W S F M H Z H E W T B
A I I T U O A I O C A A A L
E A H C N S L N S I M H H E
C P A I U E D P I I A O C R
I E T T E U I Z L M L U A O
N R R N R B V C A A A A E L
E U E A U A E S N D N L B P
V O S M T F S I O A E T S X
E T E O L R R R J K W W S E
T T D R U I S U O I R U C F
M O R O C C O E L G N U J I
D U B A I A F O R E I G N J
D E G Y P T R A V E L T N I
```

Solution on Page 325

AWNING

BED

CAMP

CARAVAN

COMFORT

DINETTE

DOOR

DRIVE

EXPLORE

FAMILY

FUN

HEATER

HIGHWAY

HITCH

HYBRID

JAUNT

KITCHEN

LIGHTS

LOST

MAP

MOBILE

OCEAN

OUTING

PARK

RELAX

ROAD

ROUTE

SHOWER

SLEEP

STARS

SUMMER

TOW

TRAVEL

TREK

TRIP

TRUCK

UNWIND

VOYAGE

WATER

WHEELS

```
L M Z O L B I W O T X B E E
Q A K Q O S R H E A T E R G
H P L I S E L E L D O O R A
W I M E T L K E R T L R G Y
S A T A V C R L E P H H M O
V U W C C A H S X P O O H V
E X M O H P R E D E B F Y U
T T D M J G X T N I G A B E
U R R F E A S T L N W M R U
O U G O P R U E I H D I I J
R C A R A V A N G E R L D K
B K E T R D W I T L I Y N Z
F J S A K A H D G G V J I B
T R I P N U F B H M E G W I
I R A W V O U T I N G W N Q
H I K I D F S H O W E R U Y
```

Solution on Page 326

AMERICAN	LUNCH
AVOCADO	MAYO
BBQ	MEAL
BEEF	MUSTARD
BIG MAC	ONION
BROILED	PATTY
BUN	PICKLE
CHEESE	PICNIC
CLASSIC	RARE
COW	RELISH
DINER	ROLL
DOUBLE	ROUND
FOOD	SANDWICH
FRY	SLIDERS
GERMANY	SUMMER
GOURMET	TOMATO
GREASY	TOPPINGS
GRILL	TURKEY
HOT	
JUICY	
KETCHUP	
LETTUCE	

```
J H N K Y R Y W G R R M I M
L W O C M T C L O D G C H E
Y S I T P U H C T E K D C A
K U N T K S E W L C L R N L
J M O D I N E R U A P A U E
S M Q L U L S S R M S T L T
F E E B K E E O L G A S L T
E R S C B E U X N I N U I U
J L I C I N C I P B D M R C
Z P B O D Q P Y R F W E G E
M Q Y U D P N D E L I O R B
R A O F O A M E R I C A N S
M J O T M D C V R A H R B F
G O U R M E T O T A M O T S
D Y E K R U T R V J R O L L
Y G C P A T T Y S A E R G E
```

ARTS

BARBECUE

BEER

BOOTHS

CAKE

CARNIVAL

CHILDREN

CIRCUS

CITY

COMMUNITY

CONTESTS

COSTUMES

CULTURAL

DANCING

EVENT

FAIR

FAMILY

FEAST

FIESTA

FIREWORKS

FOOD

FUN

GALA

GAMES

HARVEST

HOLIDAY

JUBILEE

MUSIC

PAGEANT

PARADE

SEASONAL

SHOWS

SPONSOR

SPRING

STREET

SUMMER

TICKET

TOWN

VENDORS

WINE

```
R T S A E F C Z F A M I L Y
T B E S O P V O G E E K A C
S F A K A F I E S T A M N H
U O C R C E V E N T Z F O S
M O A O B I B H I D U F S P
M D R W M E T Q O N O M A O
E E N E E M C H I L D R E N
R E I R W M U U Z C I D S S
I L V I I U B N E O A D P O
R I A F N S P R I N G T A R
T B L R E I J S C T S E G Y
O U S M U C H I I E Y E E G
W J A W I T N Q V S S R A A
N G U T O G L R O T L T N L
G G Y O X H A U R S X S T A
A A B H C H S A C I R C U S
```

Solution on Page 326

AUTOMOBILE

BATTERY

CAR

CELL

CHARGE

CLEAN

COMMUTE

COST

DESIGN

DISTANCE

DRIVE

EFFICIENT

EMISSIONS

EXPENSIVE

FUEL

FUTURE

GREEN

HYBRID

MOTOR

NEW

NISSAN

OUTLET

PLUG

POLLUTION

POWER

PRIUS

QUIET

RANGE

SCOOTER

SMALL

SOLAR

SPEED

TAXES

TESLA

TORQUE

TOYOTA

TRAIN

TRUCK

VAN

VOLT

Go Electric

```
S N D X Z D E E P S E X A T
T U G E V I S N E P X E N L
O R U F V G R A N G E I Z O
B P A F R A F U E L S H V V
N O I I S S N O I S S I M E
E W H C N C P B A W T N T G
E E V I R D O N A O F U U R
R R L E M M L O R T M W L A
G D U N O T L Q T M T D P H
R S E T E Q U J O E I E Y C
K A U S U E T C N S R B R G
C A L I I F I O T L R N U Y
U A E O R G O A Y I L L E C
R T L M S P N D D O P A B W
T N A E L C X M R O T O M Z
C O S T E L T U O I C A R S
```

Solution on Page 326

ACTIVITY

BALL

BICYCLE

BOYS

BUBBLES

CHASE

CHILDREN

CLIMB

EXERCISE

FIELD

FITNESS

FREE TIME

FRESH AIR

FRIENDS

GAMES

GIRLS

GLIDER

HANG

HIDE

HOP

JUMP

KITE

LAUGHTER

LOUD

MEMORIES

OUTDOORS

PARK

PLAYTIME

RINGS

RUN

SANDBOX

SEESAW

SKATE

SKIP

SLIDE

SOCCER

SPORTS

SUN

SWING

TEAM

```
R E C C O S E L B B U B P M
G M A E T L G M H G N S T X
N H U R C L F R I E N D S E
I O O Y I C Z S D T P A R K
W P C D S K A T E F Y L H J
S I E E F I E L D M Y A L U
B R X J D F S S D T A U L M
I H O N E R D L I H C G A P
J T B O S E I V R C L H B F
O O D B D E I A J I R T S I
S G N I R T I Z H U G E S T
E S A H C I U R L S E R X N
E D S A P M S O O S E R U E
E T I K I E U B A M Y R B S
G L U L K D N W T M E O F S
I C B L S W L K C L I M B O
```

Solution on Page 327

ADVICE

AMENITIES

AWARE

BARGAINS

BOOK

BROCHURE

CAR

CONTACT

COST

CRUISE

DEALS

DISCOUNT

DOCUMENTS

EUROPE

FARES

FEES

FLIGHT

GUIDE

HELP

HOTEL

INSURANCE

ITINERARY

LODGING

MAP

MEETING

MOTEL

OFFICE

PACKAGE

PAMPHLET

PASSPORT

PERKS

PLAN

RATES

RENTAL

RESORTS

SCHEDULE

TICKETS

TOURS

TRAIN

TRIP

```
B G U I D E E T G I B H N O
E N N C R E N T A L E T O M
R B T I C K E T S R U O T S
U P T I T P A M P H L E T E
H S F F E E S L O D G I N G
C F E L U D E H C S P N U A
O F L I G H T M A P E Y O K
R P C M T B E S I U R C C C
B A R G A I N S N A K O S A
R S F P E C N A R U S N I P
Y S D O C U M E N T S T D F
E P O R U E N S M D E A L S
R O A D V I C E E A P C E E
A R L S T R O S E R L T T T
W T N I A R T R I P A O O A
A C W K I S B O O K N F H R
```

Solution on Page 327

BEAUTY

BEDFORD

CAMDEN

CARS

CITY

COSTLY

CULTURE

DINING

EVENTS

FAME

FANCY

FASHION

GALA

GARDENS

GLAMOUR

HAUGHTY

HOMES

JEWELS

LAVISH

LEGENDS

LEISURE

LOADED

LUSH

LUXURY

MANSION

MONEY

MOVIES

PARKS

POOLS

POSH

PRIVATE

RICH

RITZY

SALON

STARS

STORE

SWANK

TOUR

TRENDY

WEALTH

```
U C S D N E G E L A V I S H
W R N O I S N A M F A M E O
H T Y Z T I R H R S C X V K
P K E Z H K A Y W D R B E N
S A N S C U L T U R E A N A
L E O Z G T A P Z D T N T W
O P M H S L G N F C A R S S
O E T O U E E O W L V F E T
P Y C S H I R I T U I C I O
D E H S K D U H S X R A V R
D E H K B J O S T U P M O E
D Y D R F E M A F R R D M O
H T L A E W A F K Y E E Z H
S I N P O E L U G N I N I D
H C I R J L G L T O U R D L
Y N O L A S M R M Y V O G Y
```

Solution on Page 327

AIMLESS	RELAX
AMBLING	ROAD
ANYWHERE	SCENIC
ASPHALT	SEAT
BYWAY	SEDAN
CAR	SIGNS
COUNTRY	SINGING
COUPLE	SLOW
EASY	STOPS
ENJOY	TOURING
FARMS	TRAVEL
FRIENDS	TREES
GAS	TRIP
GRASS	TRUCKS
HILLS	VALLEYS
JOURNEY	VIEW
LEISURE	WHIM
MILES	WINDOWS
MORNING	
MUSIC	
OUTING	
PICNIC	

```
B T O L V T R U C K S A G M
X A D X P I R T Y S A E G A
V E S A B Y W A Y M I S N V
Q S W L A Z K Q V E Y G I B
Z S S E L M I A Q E N E N F
R A G R R I B W L T L J R S
N R N E H O H L L S R I O L
C G I H O I A A I G E E M Y
O O T W M V H D L N M L E X
U S U Y N P A E D I G X I S
P M O N S A I S C G N R F M
L U Q A T S D I O N I V A P
E S J O U R N E Y I R I R C
H I G R P C Y J S S U E M D
S C E N I C W I N D O W S R
C Y S P O T S L O W T J P F
```

Solution on Page 327

ASIA

ATHENS

BAHAMAS

BEACH

BERLIN

CAVES

CITIES

COUNTRY

CRUISE

DESERT

DIVING

DUBAI

ENGLAND

EXOTIC

GIZA

HAWAII

HOTEL

IRELAND

ISLAND

JUNGLE

LAKE

LONDON

MALDIVES

MONACO

MOUNTAIN

MUSEUMS

NEW YORK

OCEAN

ORLANDO

PARK

RESORT

ROME

SCOTLAND

SPA

SYDNEY

TOKYO

TORONTO

TROPICS

VEGAS

VENICE

```
Y D U B A I S L A N D B K C
E S B E A C H A W A I I I E
N M E M U S E U M S V T Q A
D C R E S O R T C D I H Z F
Y A L E T O H O N E N I G O
S C I P O R T A S S G G Y S
V R N S O L L A T E P K S E
V U W M A E M O L R O A R V
E I E N R A R G V T O A Z A
N S D I H O N E Y D M T F C
I E E A N U G R P N O H N I
C W B T J A T N A A N E O T
E L O N S N E O R L A N D O
P A U U U O S C K G C S N X
R K R O Y W E N O N O T O E
E E C M A L D I V E S N L O
```

Solution on Page 328

BEVERAGE

BILL

BRUNCH

CALL

CART

CHECK

CHOOSE

COFFEE

DELIVER

DESSERT

DINNER

DISHES

DRINK

EAT

EGGS

ENJOY

FOOD

FRUIT

GUEST

HOTEL

ICE

KNOCK

LUNCH

LUXURY

MENU

MIDNIGHT

NAPKINS

ONLINE

ORDER

PASTA

PHONE

RELAX

RESORT

RESTAURANT

SALAD

SERVER

SNACK

TIP

TRAY

VARIETY

```
A D S L S Y I I R K I G C N
G R O G U P H O N E W Q A U
C D G O K N H O H T N P L N
H E E F F O C K D C K N L E
E W Q S H K T H G I N D I M
C H O O S E N T N U S U S D
K D Z J I E A S R A E H R I
D E L I V E R T E A T S E B
A N V J A D U T L R Y T T S
L I T A W Y A J A H V J O N
A L D L R K T C X P O E C A
S N H U N I S R F P L T R C
B O X I O B E V E R A G E K
I U R E S O R T X D U S P L
L D C Q E N J O Y S R I T K
L I U F H I A B H B B T O T A
```

Solution on Page 328

BOND ISSUES

BUSINESS LOOPS

CONCRETE

CONSTRUCTION

DEFENSE

EISENHOWER

EXIT NUMBERS

FEDERAL

FINANCING

FREEWAYS

INTERCHANGE

MAP

MEDIAN

MILES

NATION

NETWORK

PAVEMENT

PAVING

PUBLIC WORKS

ROUTE

RURAL

SIGNAGE

SPEED LIMITS

SPURS

STANDARDS

TAXES

TOLLS

TRANSPORTATION

TWO LANES

UNDERPASSES

```
S P E E D L I M I T S P R Y
H E I S E N H O W E R A U W
S S F W S E L I M B E V R S
K L E D P E T U O R B I A D
R L D E O T M N N E M N L R
O O E F O G D D O G U G T A
W T R E L I C E I N N N W D
T R A N S P O R T A T I O N
E F L S S A N P C H I C L A
N R U E E V C A U C X N A T
G E M G N E R S R R E A N S
S E E A I M E S T E M N E P
E W D N S E T E S T A I S U
X A I G U N E S N N P F R R
A Y A I B T L N O I T A N S
T S N S K R O W C I L B U P
```

Solution on Page 328

BARGE

BLUEGRASS

BNSF RAILWAY

BOONE COUNTY

BOWLING GREEN

BULLITT COUNTY

CARDINAL

CLOGGING

COAL

COVINGTON

DAVIESS COUNTY

ELIZABETHTOWN

FAYETTE COUNTY

FRANKFORT

HARDIN COUNTY

HIGH BRIDGE

HONEYBEE

JEFFERSONTOWN

KENTON COUNTY

LOUISVILLE

MURRAY STATE

NICHOLASVILLE

WARREN COUNTY

```
S E L L I V S A L O H C I N
Y W Y A W L I A R F S N B W
N T T O O E E B Y E N O H O
Y T N U O C E T T E Y A F T
T Y U U B O T L N H G K S H
N T O Y O U A O U I N R S T
U N C T W C T U O G O L A E
O U T R L L S I C H T A R B
C O T O I O Y S N B G N G A
E C I F N G A V E R N I E Z
N N L K G G R I R I I D U I
O O L N G I R L R D V R L L
O T U A R N U L A G O A B E
B N B R E G M E W E C C D E
J E F F E R S O N T O W N C
M K Y T N U O C N I D R A H
```

Solution on Page 328

ANGUILLA

ANTIGUA

ANTILLES

ARCHIPELAGO

ARUBA

BAHAMAS

BARBADOS

BARBUDA

BELIZE

BERMUDA

BIODIVERSITY

CAYS

DOMINICA

FISH

GRENADA

GUYANA

HAITI

HURRICANE

KINGSTON

MARTINIQUE

MONTSERRAT

NEVIS

REEFS

SAINT LUCIA

SAINT MARTIN

SAN JUAN

SANTO DOMINGO

SNORKELING

SURINAME

TROPICAL

WEST INDIES

Caribbean Vacation

```
R O B D S T A D U M R E B H
E W A O Y A B B A H A M A S
E E R M A R T I N I Q U E X
F S C I C R Y R C S L L S S
S T H N A E E U I A L A A U
O I I I D S L V C I N N I R
D N P C A T E I T T J S N I
A D E A N N P N O U N F T N
B I L I E O A D A O I I M A
R E A S R M O N R S A G A M
A S G T G M U K H H B U R E
B I O D I V E R S I T Y T Z
U S O N A L L I U G N A I I
R W G K I N G S T O N N N L
A O E N A C I R R U H A Q E
A U G I T N A D U B R A B B
```

ADMISSIONS

BEVERAGES

CAR

DOCUMENTS

DRINKS

EMERGENCIES

FEE

FLIGHT

FOOD

GAS

GIFTS

GUIDES

HOTEL

INCIDENTALS

INSURANCE

LAUNDRY

LODGING

MAPS

MEALS

MILEAGE

MOTEL

PARKING

PASSPORT

PHONE

RENTAL

RESORT

ROOM

SHIPPING

SHOPPING

SHUTTLES

SNACKS

SOUVENIR

TAXI

TIP

TOLLS

TOURS

TRAIN

VALET

VISA

WARDROBE

```
F N I A R T O M O T E L A V R
R D E B O R D R A W R O O M
T Y I M I L E A G E I X A T
O R I N E V U O S N A C K S
L D G G T R O P S S A P I T
L N N F U D G N I P P O H S
S U I N C I D E N T A L S S
T A K S K E D G N W G E F E
F L R H T C A E A C N L T G
I A A U S N O I S S I M D A
G T P T K A E T T G G E A R
F N H T N R O M H R D A S E
O E O L I U X T U A O L I V
O R N E R S P A M C L S V E
D U E S D N K L E T O H E B
E F Y G N I P P I H S D Z R
```

Solution on Page 329

ARBORETUM

BEAUTIFUL

BLOOMS

BOTANY

BULBS

CACTI

DISPLAYS

EDUCATION

EXHIBITS

EXOTIC

FLOWERS

GARDENS

GREENHOUSE

GROW

HERBS

HOT

LANDSCAPE

LATIN

MEDICINAL

NAMES

NATURE

ORCHIDS

PARKS

PLANTS

PUBLIC

RARE

RESEARCH

ROSES

SCIENCE

SEEDS

SHRUBS

SPECIES

STEM

STUDY

SUCCULENTS

TOURS

TREES

TROPICS

VISITORS

WATER

```
O C S P E C I E S B U R H S
E B M W I P Y N A T O B M J
V N O T U B E A U T I F U L
V R O B S D I H C R O S T P
G X L G R E E N H O U S E L
E I B A E Y S C A C T I R A
C S G T W E D U C A T I O N
S K B V O E R U T A N L B T
R R U I L H L A T I N A R S
U A L S F E P A C S D N A L
O P B I N S Y A L P S I D R
T W S T I B I H X E D C F O
R A S O R A R E C N E I C S
E T T R O P I C S N E D J E
E E E S V H C R A E S E R S
S R M H E R B S Z S E M A N
```

Solution on Page 329

ACCIDENT

ADVISORY

ALERT

AVOID

BLOCKAGE

BRIDGE

BYPASS

CAMERA

CLOSED

COLLISION

COMMUTE

CONES

CRASH

CREW

CROSSWALK

DEBRIS

DELAY

DETOUR

DRIVE

FLOODING

HAZARDS

HIGHWAY

ICE

INTERSECTION

OBSTRUCTIONS

OVERPASS

PARKING

PATROL

REPORT

REROUTED

ROAD

RUSH

SLOW

STEADY

STOP

TIME

UNDERPASS

WARNINGS

WEATHER

WRECK

```
K E M I T C C L M T H S U R
C S G Y N O D O K B R D W A
E D N R E M E R L L E E O H
R R I O D M S T A O R L L S
W A D S I U O A W C O A S A
E Z O I C T L P S K U Y T R
A A O V C E C G S A T S O C
T H L D A O R U O G E E P W
H D F A S S A P R E D N U A
E I N T E R S E C T I O N R
R O G O V E R P A S S C P N
U V A H V U E G D I R B E I
O A N I W C O L L I S I O N
T A R E M A C P A R K I N G
E D S S A P Y B D E B R I S
D R E P O R T Y D A E T S S
```

Solution on Page 329

ALPINE

BOARD

BOOTS

BUNNY

CABIN

CARVE

CHALET

COAT

COLD

DRIFTS

FIRE

FLIGHT

FUN

GEAR

GLOVES

HELMET

HILLS

HOTEL

JUMP

LEASH

LIFT

LODGE

MASK

NORDIC

PARKA

POLE

POWDER

RACE

RESORT

SKIS

SLALOM

SLED

SLOPE

SNOW

SUIT

SUMMIT

THRILL

TRAIL

TREES

TRIP

```
Z A H J B S E F R O F H E F
T A I U Y L N L D I H G G X
Q T L M O H D I V R D E W V
Y I L P G R L G S O A P F Y
Q M S I I C O H L R J O M B
B M B F F N C T O O T W B N
E U T O O T E R P R V D E J
V S N R O L F H E L M E T W
R W D N A T K E S S N R S H
A I D H Y I S L A L O M J O
C T C P W F A C L L I R H T
V A I I O V M M O D I P T E
S R B U N D F R E H S A E L
T S K I S U X K A L O R R M
T O Y E N E B U E C Z K I T
F R V U O R I D D A E A F Z
```

Solution on Page 330

AIRPORT	PASS
BAGS	PATROL
BELONGINGS	PERMIT
BORDER	PHOTO
CUSTOMS	POLICE
DETAIN	PROTECT
DETECTOR	QUESTION
DOCUMENTS	RANDOM
DOGS	SAFE
DOMESTIC	SCAN
EXAMINE	SCREENING
FLIGHTS	SEARCH
GATE	STAMP
GUARD	TICKETS
HIDDEN	TRAVEL
JAIL	WAND
LAW	WATCH
LICENSE	WEAPONS
LINES	
LIQUIDS	
METAL	
OFFICER	

```
W W A T C H I D D E N K T C
A Y L L E V A R T I M R E P
N F I L L O R T A P L W H M
D A P N S M O T S U C E C A
J P R O T C E T E D N A R T
T H O I C D R B S S A P E S
R O T T S T N E M U C O D G
N T E S E I Z L E N S N R A
E O C E A C A O X N D S O B
E F T U R K I N A R I E B E
Q F L Q C E R G M A U N I T
Y I A I H T P I I N Q I G A
F C T S G S O N N D I L U G
J E E Y H H R G E O L W A L
P R M F C I T S E M O D R J
P O L I C E N S E S G O D G
```

Solution on Page 330

BED	MEALS
BLANKET	OVERNIGHT
BREAKFAST	PARTY
CLEANING	PLEASANT
COMMOTION	ROOM
COMPANY	SCHEDULE
COOKING	SHEETS
DINNER	SHOWER
ENJOY	SNACKS
ENTERTAIN	SUPPER
FAMILY	TOWELS
FOOD	TRAVEL
FRIEND	TRIP
FUN	UNWANTED
GAMES	VACATION
GIFT	VISITOR
HOLIDAYS	WELCOME
HOSTING	
ITINERARY	
LAUNDRY	
LINENS	
MATTRESS	

```
O Q S K C A N S L A E M Z N
S C H E D U L E M O C L E W
D S E S M I V C O O K I N G
P L E A S A N T T R I P U N
D I T R R L G N O C B P F I
N N S T T E N T E R T A I N
E E L B I T I N E R A R Y A
I N C X L S A A M B O L Y E
R S O F I A K M S O I O D L
F G M V O F N Y M M J E L C
P N M C A O A K A N T S A O
A I O S W D D F E N G H U M
R T T T I V A C A T I O N P
T S I L S L E W O T F W D A
Y O O V E R N I G H T E R N
B H N O S U P P E R B R Y Y
```

Solution on Page 330

BARRE

BENNINGTON

BRATTLEBORO

BURLINGTON

CAMELS HUMP

CHIMNEY POINT

COLCHESTER

DAIRY

DERBY

ESSEX

FORT DUMMER

FORT MOTT

KILLINGTON

LINCOLN PEAK

LYNDON

MAPLE

MILTON

MOUNT ABRAHAM

MOUNT ELLEN

NEW ENGLAND

NORTHFIELD

PICO PEAK

QUARRYING

SEASONAL

SKI

SPRINGFIELD

ST JOHNSBURY

SWANTON

```
S P R I N G F I E L D T A P
D K M A H A R B A T N U O M
M N O T G N I L L I K E R U
B E N N I N G T O N O L O H
L I N C O L N P E A K P B S
R D O T C D Y X I K G A E L
E L T T Y E R E K A N M L E
T E G O N R U S S E I O T M
S I N M O B B S W P Y U T A
E F I T D Y S E A O R N A C
H H L R N Y N Y N C R T R M
C T R O Y G H R T I A E B I
L R U F L G O I O P U L A L
O O B A R S J A N Z Q L R T
C N N F O R T D U M M E R O
A D L A N O S A E S G N E N
```

Solution on Page 330

BATH	MOTEL
BED	PAD
CAMPER	PILLOW
CARAVAN	POOL
CHALET	RANCH
CLUB	RENTAL
COTTAGE	RESORT
CRIB	ROOM
FAN	SERVICE
FLOOR	SHACK
GYM	SHELTER
HEATER	SHOWER
HOSTEL	SUITE
HOTEL	TENT
HOUSE	TOWEL
HUT	VALET
INN	VILLA
LAMPS	YACHT
LOBBY	
LODGE	
MAID	
MANAGER	

```
R Y C B E D G T V P M A V S
W A B L S O Q E U A E L Z B
F A N B U L H N K S Z L H R
B N M C O B A T H W K H O H
I P A D H L R O O L F O U F
T L G K A A W L S A M T X N
Q E X T C E L D S M E E S B
M W L R R I Y E H P B L B L
D O N A P O C O T S A M I A
I T Q A V I S L E T O M R U
A L L I V T H E N G C B C G
M R W R E A G E R T H C A Y
S H E L T E R E G A N A M M
B S O I I E G A T T O C P E
F O W V U N Y K C A H S E U
P N F K S K X H E A T E R T
```

Solution on Page 331

ACQUA ALTA

ADRIATIC

ARCHITECTURE

ARTWORKS

BOAT

BRIDGES

CANNAREGIO

CASTELLO

COMUNE

CULTURAL

DORSODURO

FILM FESTIVAL

FLOOD

GIUDECCA

GONDOLA

HUMID

ISLANDS

LA FENICE

LAGOON

LIDO

MARCO POLO

OPERA

PELLESTRINA

PIAVE RIVER

PO RIVER

SAN MARCO

SAN POLO

SANTA CROCE

SESTIERI

SHAKESPEARE

TIDES

VENETI

WATER

```
S D N A L S I R E I T S E S
G F S H A K E S P E A R E E E
O I A D R I A T I C U O W G
N L A N G L S I U T E P A D
D M I C I G A D C N C I T I
O F C D Q R N E A O I A E R
L E A J O U T S S O N V R B
A S N K M I A S T G E E E O
C T N U H A C A E A F R V L
C I A C M M R U L L A I I O
E V R O O O O C L T L V R P
D A E R B P C K O T A E O N
U L G V E N E T I P U R P A
I D I M U H A R T W O R K S
G Q O C R A M N A S D L A P
F L O O D O R S O D U R O L
```

Solution on Page 331

ANIMAL

BEECH

BIOME

BRANCHES

CANOPY

DECIDUOUS

DRY

ECOLOGY

ECOSYSTEM

FALL

FIRE

FOLIAGE

FORESTRY

FUNGI

GREEN

GROVE

HABITAT

HUNTING

INSECTS

LEAF

LOST

MOSS

MOUNTAINS

NATIONAL

NATURE

OAK

OUTSIDE

PINE

PLANTS

RAIN

ROOTS

SOIL

SWAMP

TENT

TIMBER

TREE

TROPICAL

WATER

WILD

WOOD

```
Q H O A N D O H G R E E N M
D M L Y P O N A C B D O O W
P E S L L B H B K E I S O I
P M R X A P U I Z E S N M N
C L A U N F N T G C T O J S
W A R W T X T A M H U A E E
Z M S E S A I T E N O M V C
H I E U B L N X T B V L O T
S N H T O M G A S R I I R S
R A C F E U I W Y O A O G K
Y T N P W N D T S F P I M E
G I A U S S T I O I P I N E
F O R E S T R Y C R G L K R
Y N B T S O L A E E V N N T
R A W E C O L O G Y D L U F
D L I W W R E T A W L E A F
```

Solution on Page 331

ALCOHOL

ANTE

BANKROLL

BET

BINGO

BLACKJACK

CARD

CASH

CHIPS

COMPS

CRAPS

DEALER

DICE

DRINKING

FUN

GAME

JACKPOTS

JUNKET

KENO

LADY LUCK

LAS VEGAS

LOSERS

LOSING

MAXIMUM

MINIMUM

MONEY

ODDS

PARTY

PAYOFF

PIT BOSS

PLAYER

POKER

RISK

ROULETTE

SHUFFLE

SLOT

TABLE

VIDEO

WAGER

WIN

```
A J F X G A M E V E L B A T
Q G M U M I X A M U O K E E
S T E K N U J L M H S A C L
R G N I S O L C A I E Q I F
K S M E O D Q O R Q R V D F
I U D E E D C H I P S K P U
M B I R D S S O B T I P K H
F O G N I B S L O T R C C S
E F M Z V N N P N H U Z A P
Y T O B A N K R O L L G J M
U P N Y R C D I Y K E E K O
P L E A A E S D N V E K C C
H A Y J A P A P S G E R A A
B Y R L R L F A A N I W L R
U E E T T E L U O R D Z B D
C R T D Y R E G A W C C R U
```

Solution on Page 331

AFRICA

ANGKOR

ANTARCTICA

ARGENTINA

ASIA

BRAZIL

CANADA

CARIBBEAN

CHINA

DOVER

EGYPT

ENGLAND

EUROPE

FRANCE

GERMANY

GIZA

GREECE

HONG KONG

INDIA

IRELAND

ITALY

KILIMANJARO

KUWAIT

MADAGASCAR

MEXICO

NIGERIA

NORTH AMERICA

NORTH POLE

PANAMA

PORTUGAL

SCOTLAND

SOUTH AMERICA

SOUTH POLE

THAILAND

VIETNAM

```
N L A G U T R O P A I S A Y
G E T C A R O K G N A C Z L
R P G H I F A I D N I O I A
E O S E A R R L T R D T G T
E R G J R I E I E J A L S I
C U N L G M L M C M A A O M
E E O I E W A A A A C N U A
K N K Z N H D N N H I D T D
U G G A T T A J Y D T E H A
W L N R I P N A N O C U P G
A A O B N Y A R I V R F O A
I N H X A G C O G E A R L S
T D N A L E R I E R T A E C
X Y E L O P H T R O N N O A
C H I N A E B B I R A C A R
G C O C I X E M A N T E I V
```

Solution on Page 332

ADVICE

AIR BAG

ALERT

ATTENTIVE

BUCKLE

CARE

CAUTION

CONSCIOUS

CUSTOMS

DOCUMENTS

DRIVE

EMBASSY

EMERGENCY

FIRST AID

GROUP

HEEDFUL

HIGHWAYS

HOTEL

LAWS

LIGHTS

MONEY

NEWS

PHONE

PLAN

POLICE

PRUDENCE

REPORTS

RESEARCH

ROADS

RULES

SCAM

SCHEDULE

SECURITY

SIGNS

SWINDLER

TICKETS

TOUR

TROOPER

WARY

WEATHER

```
D I M A C S T O U R U L E S
H E E D F U L I G H T S D D
P O L I C E N O I T U A C A
A S Y A W H G I H O T E L O
N L K T R Y S W I N D L E R
B S E S S N E C N E D U R P
U T U R G W S C S E R A C R
C E V I T N E T T A I K E E
K K S F O E N N T S V S L H
L C Y C N E G R E M E M U T
E I C O M A O C N A M O D A
C T H U B O U P R N B T E E
I P C R P R U C A P A S H W
V O I E I O H L A W S U C R
D A R T R E P O R T S C S L
A T Y G S F M O N E Y R A W
```

Solution on Page 332

BAYFRONT PARK

BRICKELL KEY

CLEAN

COCONUT GROVE

CRUISE SHIPS

CULTURE

EL JARDIN

FINANCE

FLAGLER STREET

FLORIDA

FREEDOM TOWER

GREEN SPACES

HAHN BUILDING

HALISSEE HALL

LYRIC THEATER

MIAMI HERALD

OMNI

PALM COTTAGE

PARK WEST

RICHEST

SIMPSON PARK

SOUTHSIDE PARK

VIZCAYA

Solution on Page 322

```
U S E C A P S N E E R G F F
M I A M I H E R A L D L L R
S O Y G F L O R I D A Y V E
L O C O C O N U T G R O V E
K L U S P U O V L I C A S D
P R A T P A L E C N L R I O
A E A H H I R T R M E I M M
L Y L P E S H K U O A C P T
M H J J T E I S W R N H S O
C I M R A N S D E E E E O W
O P E T Y R O S E S S S N E
T E E B P Q D R I P I T P R
T R E C N A N I F L A U A Y
A Y A C Z I V V N Y A R R S
G N I D L I U B N H A H K C
E Y E K L L E K C I R B J T
```

Solution on Page 332

ANTIQUES

BRANDS

CARS

CHROME

CLASSIC

COMPANIES

CONCEPT

CROWD

CUSTOM

DEBUT

DESIGN

DETAILED

DISPLAY

DREAM

ENGINE

EXHIBIT

EXPENSIVE

EXPERTS

FUN

IMPORTS

LIGHTS

LINE

LUXURY

MAKE

MODEL

PEOPLE

PISTONS

RIMS

ROTORS

SHOP

SPEAKERS

STAGE

TICKETS

TROPHIES

TRUCK

TURBO

USHERS

VANS

VEHICLE

VINTAGE

Solution on Page

```
R O T O R S M O D E L I N E
Q N R R N M P I S T O N S K
O G U V O I M P O R T S Z A
B I C A T P E N G I N E V M
R S K N N A H C H R O M E S
U E S V K T L I G H T S H R
T D D E T A I L E D T S I A
Y I R Q I Z W Q T S T Y C C
R S B R A N D S U R N F L T
U P V I N T A G E E U A E P
X L U J H E X P E N S I V E
U A C S L X X U M S O R D C
L Y R P H E E D I O L I E N
Y P O S T E K C I T C M B O
M E W M A E R D M O T S U C
P Y D K P O H S R E G A T S
```

Solution on Page 332

AMAGER VEST

AMALIENBORG

BALTIC SEA

BICYCLE PATHS

CAPITAL

CULTURE

DENMARK

DIESELHOUSE

HDMS SEHESTED

HOLMENS KANAL

INDRE BY

ISLANDS BRYGGE

KASTELLET

KIERKEGAARD

LITTLE MERMAID

MAERSK

METROPOLITAN

NOMA

NYHAVN

PARKS

SCANDINAVIA

TIVOLI GARDENS

VALBY

VICTOR BORGE

VIKING

```
E A D E T S E H E S S M D H
X G E Y B V K R A M N E D T
H M R S B C I N M S E T E K
A D A O C E A K O C D R G I
M I I E B I R A I M R O G E
A E V A R R T D K N A P Y R
L S A C M S O L N M G O R K
I E N U N R K T A I I L B E
E L I L Y S E G C B L I S G
N H D T H K E M L I O T D A
B O N U A R A L E G V A N A
O U A R V A L B Y L I N A R
R S C E N P C A P I T A L D
G E S K A S T E L L E T S A
M T S H T A P E L C Y C I B
J N H O L M E N S K A N A L
```

Solution on Page 333

ANTELOPE	LEOPARD
BUFFALO	LION
CAR	LODGE
CHEETAH	NATURE
DOCUMENT	QUEST
ECOLOGY	QUIET
EXPLORE	RHINO
FLIGHT	SNAKES
GAME	SPIDERS
GAZELLE	SUN
GIRAFFE	TOURS
GORILLA	TRAVEL
GRASS	TREK
GUN	TRIP
HAT	TRUCK
HIPPO	VIEWING
HOT	WATER
HUNT	ZEBRA
JOURNEY	
JUNGLE	
KANGAROO	
LAND	

```
L T N U H O T C W J G K H U
T J P I E J U N G L E C K C
M Q P G A Z E L L E D U V W
M P D S N Y L F E O J R I B
O O N P T G O T F P O T E M
L N M I E O L R E A U H W R
R I P D L L A I R R R G I E
A H S E O O F P O D N I N T
C R H R P C F J L N E L G A
M A B S E E U A P V Y F O W
T S K E R T B M X T O U R S
E B S K Z C H E E T A H I Y
I P K A O O R A G N A K L L
U G U N R L E V A R T N L A
Q U E S T G A M E R U T A N
O W Q J N T O P Z S O I W D
```

Solution on Page 333

ADVENTURE	NEWS
ADVICE	PEOPLE
ANECDOTES	PICTURES
ARTICLES	PLANNING
COMPANY	RATE
COUNTRY	RECORD
CUISINE	RESORT
CULTURE	REVIEWS
DESCRIBE	SCHEDULE
DISCOVERY	SHARE
EXPLORE	SPONSOR
FLIGHT	STEPS
FOOD	STOP
GEOGRAPHY	TERRAIN
HOTEL	TIDBITS
IDEAS	TIPS
JOURNAL	TOUR
LANDMARKS	
LIFESTYLE	
MAPS	
MEMORIES	
NATURE	

```
N E N I S I U C M A P S D T
E R O L P X E C O P E O T R
W U S E I R O M E M O I R O
S T E P S U N L A F P T O S
T L N T N I Y S N S L A S E
I U Q T A T H E E S E D N R
B C R R S R P R C E Y E O Y
D Y R E A U A U D R R S P U
I E F E D O R T O U E C S G
T I L E V T G A T T V R J N
L D E D I I O N E C O I O I
A R T I C L E S S I C B U N
L O O D E V G W H P S E R N
S C H E D U L E S P I Z N A
G E R A H S K R A M D N A L
G R V S F L I G H T S T L P
```

Solution on Page 333

BAGS

BEACH

BREAK

CARNIVAL

COUNTRY

COUPLE

DOWNTOWN

DRIVE

ESCAPE

EXPLORE

FAIR

FAMILY

FAST

FREEDOM

FRIENDS

GOLF

HIATUS

HOTEL

INN

LAKE

LEAVE

LOCAL

MOTEL

PACK

PARTY

PICNIC

QUICK

RELAX

REST

RETREAT

ROMANTIC

SHORT

SITTER

SPA

SURPRISE

TIME OFF

TOURIST

TRIP

VACATION

VISIT

```
Q M S R Y L I M A F L O G S
L R F X N N I D R G E H G G
N A C C F F O E M I T E B A
T M K I H W E I X R L R R B
F R I E N D S S T P E E E W
C R P T O C H R U A L A X L
A R O M Q O I O K A C O E N
R W K M R P C P X H P A R R
N H C T A E R T E R V S V E
I R C O U N T R Y E S H Y T
V E V I S I T S I R U O T T
A V S U R P R I S E T T R I
L I K C I U Q I C S A E A S
S R I L A C O L A T I L P U
L D K C A P T S A F H C G N
J Y K E W L E T O M Z R V C
```

Solution on Page 333

BEAR MOUNTAIN

BRIDGEPORT

BRISTOL

DANBURY

DUTCH

ENFIELD

GOLD COAST

HAMDEN

MANCHESTER

MARITIME

MERIDEN

MIANUS RIVER

MIDDLESEX

MOUNT FRISSELL

MYSTIC RIVER

NEW BRITAIN

NEW ENGLAND

NEW HAVEN

NIANTIC RIVER

NUTMEG STATE

SOUTHINGTON

THAMES RIVER

WALLINGFORD

WEALTHY

WINDHAM

```
Y M A R I T I M E P Q W N Y
U Z B E A R M O U N T A I N
L O T S I R B U X E S L A B
N E D M A H D N I W A L N T
S N M D Y D U T C H O I T H
O I I I R S O F Z A C N I A
U A D Y A E T R H V D G C M
T T D R N N T I J E L F R E
H I L U E F U S C N O O I S
I R E B D I W S E R G R V R
N B S N I E Z E R H I D E I
G W E A R L W L A I C V R V
T E X D E D W L G L V N E E
O N U T M E G S T A T E A R
N E W E N G L A N D T H R M
T R O P E G D I R B P Y Y X
```

Solution on Page 334

AUNT	NIECE
BARBECUE	PARTY
BIRTHDAY	PASSOVER
BOND	PICTURES
BROTHER	PLAN
CHILDREN	RELAX
DINNER	REUNION
DRIVE	SHARE
EAT	SHOWER
EMOTIONS	SIT
FAMILY	SPECIAL
FATHER	STORIES
FLY	TALK
GRANDMA	TRAVEL
GUESTS	TRIP
HOLIDAY	UNCLE
JOY	WEDDING
KIN	WEEKEND
LOVE	
MEMORIES	
MOTHER	
NEPHEW	

```
Q K A R E H T O M F T I S L
N B N E P H E W L A Q Y I G
F A T H E R C W E E K E N D
T L E T D I N N E R P I R Y
J O Y O E L C N U I D I U T
U N E R D L I H C D V S A R
J I M B A U N T E E E L Y A
N E O E T R U W B I K L Y P
E C T N E R B I R T H D A Y
R E I W E O I O A S S S D L
A K O S N N M P B T S E I I
H H N D R E U N I O N V L M
S I S E M Q H T V R F O O A
K P L A N S P E C I A L H F
L A M D N A R G U E S T S O
X L E V A R T K B S Z C U H
```

Solution on Page 334

BARGAIN

BOOKING

BUS

CAMPING

CHEAP

COACH

COST

COUPON

CRUISE

DEAL

DISCOUNT

DRIVE

FAMILY

FARE

FLIGHTS

FREEBIES

GETAWAYS

GROUP

HAGGLE

HOSTEL

HOTEL

MOTEL

NIGHT

OCCUPANT

PLAN

RATE

REBATE

REDUCED

RENTAL

SALES

SAVE

SLASHED

SPECIAL

STAY

SUBWAY

TICKETS

TOURS

TRAIN

TRIP

WALK

```
M E W A N I A R T O U R S K
H Y P C S U B D N H H H Y T L
M C N O P U O C E C G L A A
E H C A O C O G F H D I Y W
P U O R G L K L J E S M N G
G T C S G N I P M A C A A D
K L R S T G N A L P S F L I
P R U I H E G E T A W A Y S
E A I T P I L N L B E J E C
Y T S O C A A E S V E I L O
A E E Q I P S T I R B L G U
W D E C U D E R A E Q A G N
B G E C A K D F E B R T A T
U P C V C B A R G A I N H X
S O F I A Y F U J T D E A L
L E T O H S M O T E L R R V
```

Solution on Page 334

AFRICA
ALTITUDE
ARCTIC
AREA
ASIA
BORDER
BRIDGE
CITY
COAST
COUNTY
CREEK
DISCOVER
EARTH
EQUATOR
EUROPE
EXPLORE
HIGHWAY
KEY
LAND
LEGEND
MAP
NAMES

NATIONS
NEW
OCEANS
PACIFIC
PLACES
REGION
RIVER
ROADS
ROUTE
SCALE
SEAS
STATE
STRAITS
TERRAIN
TRAVEL
TRIP
WATER
WORLD

```
S E M A N N D J Y T A A C D
S N W A T E R O A D S W K R
D R A R C T I C B E O Y E S
L E G E N D V C O U N T Y N
R G Y V C K E K R R O U T E
O I P O I O R E D O D N A L
W O L C T C R E E P A I S A
K N A S Y A P R R E Y C T C
O D C I H E O C O Y S C E S
N B E D U T I T L A T I R A
Y P S A A C R Q P W I F R E
S E E U F P B A X H A I A S
T R Q B R I D G E G R C I M
A E M P I R S N O I T A N P
T S A O C T Z Q K H S P R Z
E M T R A V E L L D W X O H
```

Solution on Page 334

BELT

CLUTCH

COMMUTE

CRUISING

DOOR

DRIVEWAY

ENGINE

GAUGES

GEAR

GRILL

GUIDE

HIGHWAY

HORN

JOURNEY

KEY

KNOB

LEVER

LICENSE

LIGHT

MAP

MIRROR

MOVING

PARK

PEDALS

RADIO

RIDE

ROADS

RULES

SEAT

SIGNAL

SPEED

STEER

TIRES

TOUR

TRAVEL

TRIPS

TRUNK

TURNS

WHEELS

WINDOWS

```
F X C J P E X L O R R T U G
Y F M N G A H F N K I A O F
V R O R R I M V L L D E S I
U G A U G E S T I R E S N D
Z T Z H Q P I C G A W D R E
Y R W W K G E A H E H O U E
P A R K R N H D T G E B T P
Y V W I S E O J A C E M R S
Y E L E N W O B O L L O U D
E L S G V Y O M L U S V N A
K D I P B I M D H A R I K O
G N I S I U R C N A N N U R
E R B U T R T D D I G G E D
A O U E G U T I Q J W V I Y
K H I O L D O O R E E T S S
Y V C C T T Y S E L U R H D
```

Solution on Page 335

ADULTS

APPETIZER

ATMOSPHERE

ATTIRE

BREAD PLATE

CHAMPAGNE

CHEF

COST

COURSES

CUISINE

CULTURED

DECOR

DELICACY

DESSERT

DINING

ELEGANCE

EXCLUSIVE

EXPENSIVE

FANCY

FINE

FORMAL

LUXURIOUS

MEALS

MONEY

NAPKIN

OPULENT

QUALITY

RICH

SALAD FORK

SAUCEBOAT

SERVICE

STEAK

TABLECLOTH

TUXEDO

VIOLIN

WAITER

WEALTH

WINE

```
E T R E S S E D I N I N G U
N H T N E L U P O D E X U T
I E R I T T A O B E C U A S
W C O S T L U D A F E H C U
E E V I S N E P X E N I F O
A C X U K R O F D A L A S I
L N C C S A P P E T I Z E R
T A H U L Q S G C M F F D U
H G A L A U E H O O O A E X
R E M T E A S C R S R N L U
E L P U M L R I S P M C I L
T E A R Y I U R V H A Y C S
I Z G E H T O L C E L B A T
A J N D F Y C S E R V I C E
W O E T A L P D A E R B Y A
M V I O L I N A P K I N P K
```

Solution on Page 335

AIRLINE

ARRIVAL

BAG

BELT

BENEFITS

BOARDING

BONUS

BUSINESS

CREDITS

DEALS

DISCOUNT

ELITE

ENROLL

EXPLORER

EXTRAS

FARE

FLIGHT

FREE

GATE

HOTEL

LOYALTY

MILES

PARTNERS

PASS

PERK

PILOT

PLANS

POINTS

PROGRAM

REDEEM

RENTALS

REWARDS

SAVE

SEAT

SLEEP

STATUS

TICKETS

TRAVEL

TRIP

WINDOW

Solution on P

```
I I P O Y T L A Y O L Z F A
H B E L T F L I G H T R I P
T S D R A W E R T O L I P B
A L L O R N E L S T A T U S
M B D T H N S I G I V S N S
I O E R T B E N E F I T S R
A N A A I D O E Z N R Z S E
Q U L V C P I A E P R F X N
J S S E K Q E S R E A P S T
W L R L E X S O C D L R E R
P O I N T S G A B O I I A A
H A D R S R F A R E U N T P
Q O A N A M E E D E R N G E
G S T M I C R E D I T S T E
M K R E P W E V A S S A P R
A I M I L E S L E E P W G F
```

Solution on Page 335

Answers

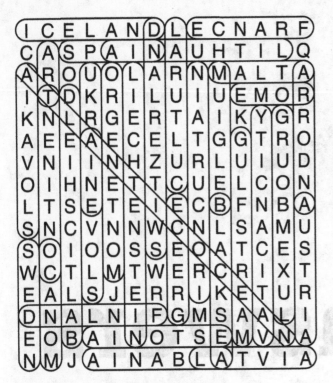

All Around Europe

Hotel Pools

Seen at a Museum

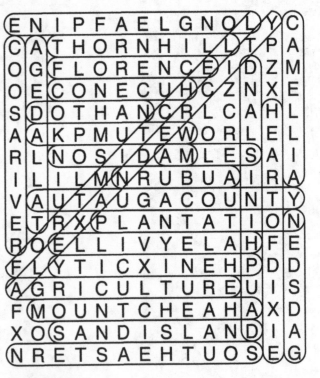

Alabama

300

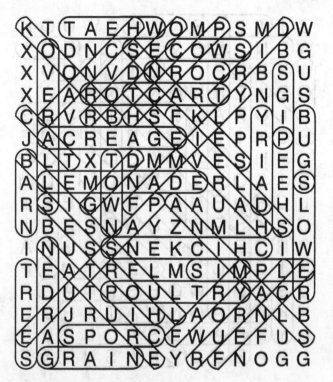

Visit the Country

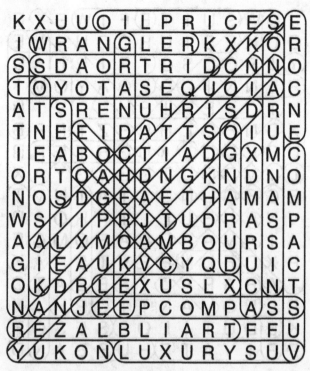

Driving an SUV

Suitcase

Reservations

Honeymoon Trip

Slick Roads

Bus Rider

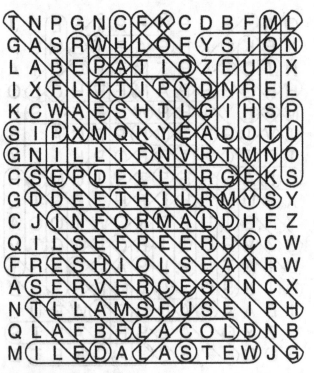

Bistros

Youth Hostel

Christmas Travel

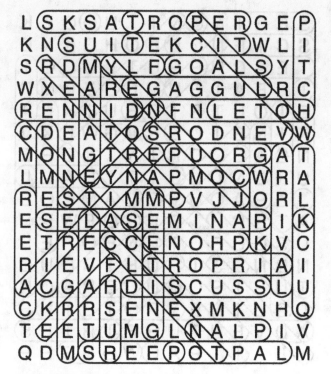

Business Trip

Michigan

Seaside

```
R E S O R T S E L A H W R I
S A N D P V M H L X I W I R
H S I F O S L D I T D O C K
S S H O R E A V E P S L O Z
T L P E T E P L H E A A N G
A O L N S W I D T M W O C S
E V O U H S U P S Y I A H U
R T D F G N B D M L C I E N
T O V E E A M O I O R E S S
E W B S H R E V A P A D E E
R E L R C V A S I T B Z A T
N L O L A P T B F E E N F I
Z C S W E H C I M F W M O D
K K Z K B H X G A V I G O E
J T T Z R S S H O T E L D H
O K N O M S U R F N A E C O
```

Car Care

```
I M U U C A V D I U L F L K
N R O T O R S T E E R I N G
S T H G I L K C E H C A A A
P Q R E T L I F S S T S E S
E E C A R B U R E T O R N K
C M C W N E A M I L E A G E
T I F I L S O T I E Z J I T
I S M P V T M N T B E S N S
O S L E O R E I C E E K E B
N I L R E N E H S E R F S Q
N O I S N E P S U S F Y O S
X N O I T I N G I A I R H E
A S A C C E L E R A T O R K
W P E A L I G N M E N T N A
C L E A N E R A D I A T O R
P O L I S H E T A T O R J B
```

Commuting

```
C E D I R P J V J Y W Z W F
G X I A R R I V A L A O V V
T T D E E F F O C F E H R N
J I K F T M R U T S C O A K
O I L H U L I E B U A M L Y
B S A G M O R T E B R E S D
U S W K M N G S W W T L P P
S E H S O G N R N A A C O F
H T D O C G I U E Y R Y T T
Q I N R R H N N W O T C S K
R C T E I T E I S T U I T F
Z K P X D V V D N C R B A C
C E A A T U E U U R H A T F
I T I R O U T E D L O O I Y
T L I Y S E S S A P E M O N
Y P V S I C K Q E U A G N L
```

School Trip

```
S E E I N G N I T U O O Z K
S C I E N C E E O H G K N B
T E A C H E R U T L U C O T
T H E A T E R M U S E U M R
E T O U T S I D E U I K E A
K I N S I D E S L G W L X V
N C A E O C P T N I X C P E
U K L N L U C I T Y H A L L
J E P A O U V O L A M C O E
A T S R H I D E P O E W R S
U S G C R U T E N E O F E S
N B N D S I R U H I R H U O
T U F T S O M U U C R A C N
L S U I N E Y R O T S I H S
A D V E N T U R E T R I P S
Y L A T I P A C W O H S H P
```

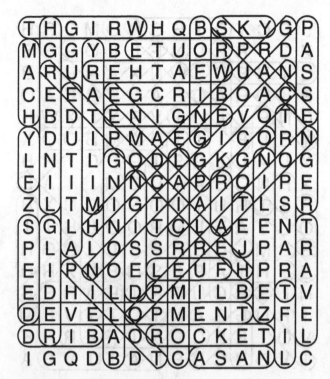

Flying Machines

Nebraska

Tourist Trap

Campground

Fun Journeys

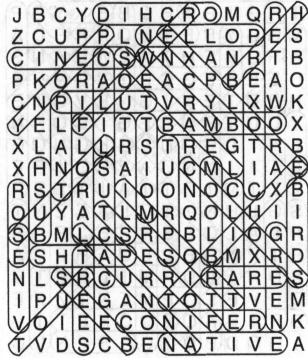

Botanical Gardens

Vacationing

Water Transportation

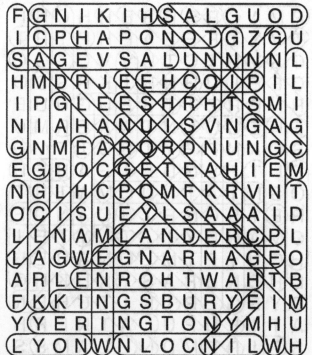

Nevada

Visit a Palace

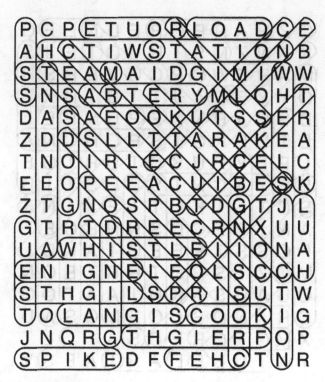

Railway

Car Repair

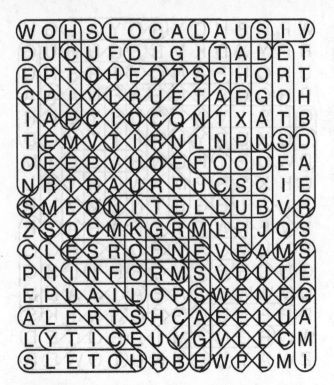

Billboards on the Road

Cabins

Macau

Boat Show

Go Whale Watching

Bridges

Road Trips

Adventure Travel

Wander Indiana

Modes of Transport

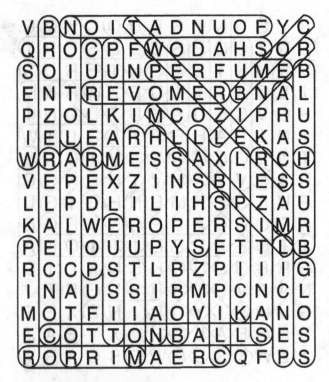

Cosmetic Bag

See the World

310

In the Wild

Bangkok

Luxury Travel

Rest Stop

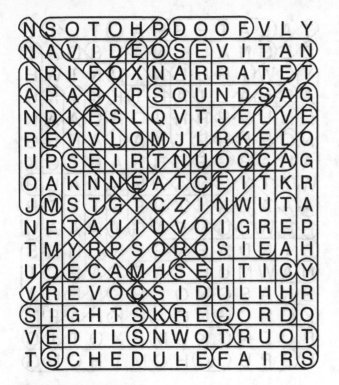

Travelogue

Grab a Doughnut

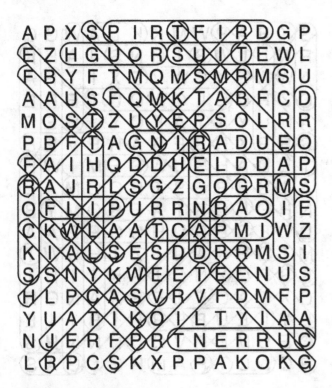

River Rafting

Bed and Breakfast

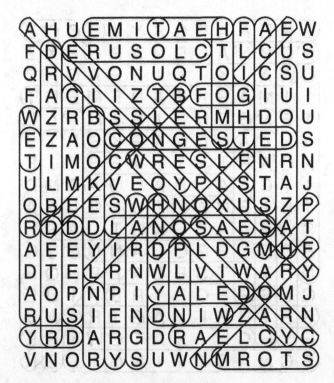

Travel Conditions

Pack a Snack

Biking

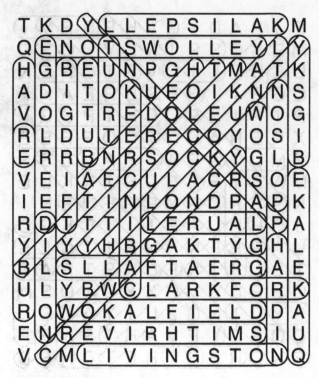

Montana

Houseboat

Tourist Attractions

Truck Stops

Dublin

Travel Clothes

Beach Vacation

National Parks

International Travel

Road Construction

Travel Journal

Use a Map

Car Tires

Louisiana

See a Waterfall

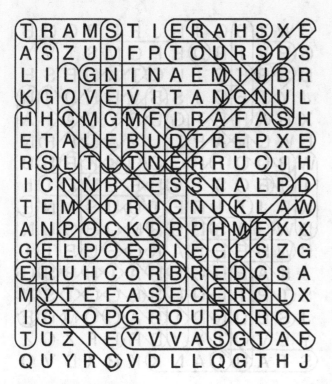

Tour Guide

Tropical Vacation

Stop for Coffee

Health Spa

Penthouse Suite

Motorbike

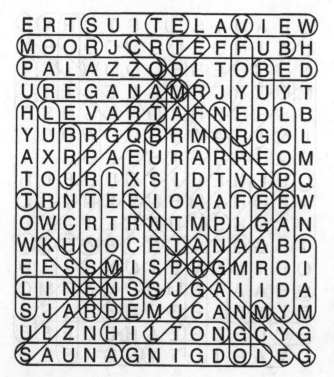

Hotels

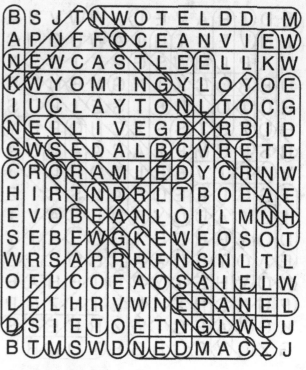

Learning a Language

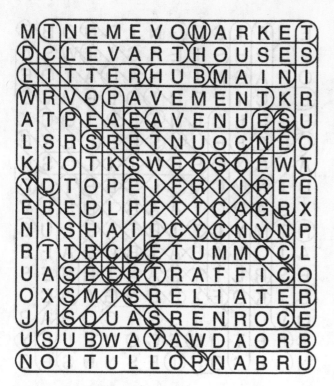

Down the Street

Delaware

Drive Safely

**Architecture
Around the U.S.**

Boat Ride

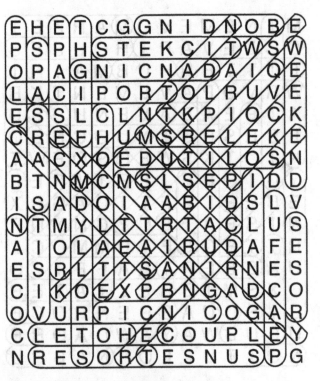

Romantic Getaway

Kansas

Driving a Volkswagen

Across the USA

Golf Trip

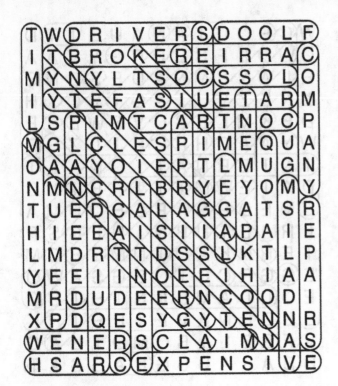

Car Insurance

Pack a Swimsuit

Iowa

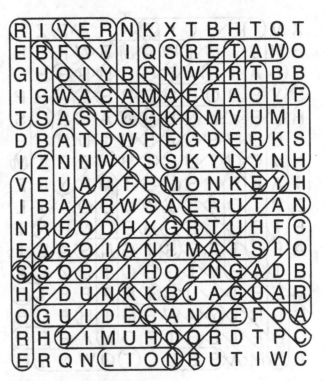

Jungle Cruise

Travel Checklist

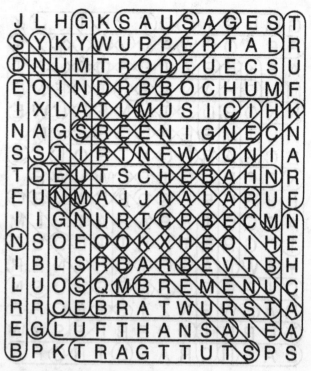

Visit Germany

Speedy Autos

Flight Time

Car Radio

Going to the Beach

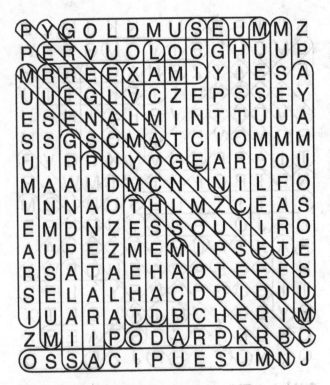

Favorite Museums

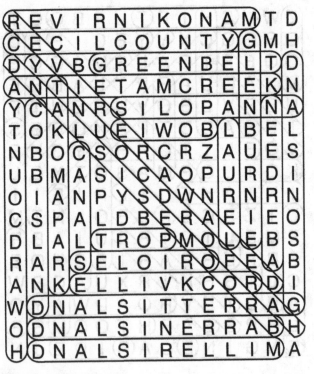

Maryland

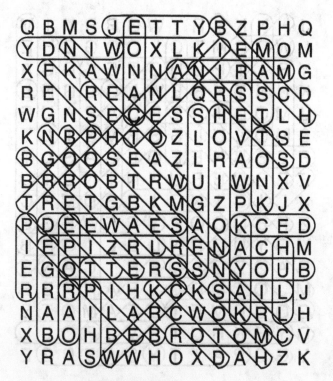

Around the Dock

Trucking

Topography

Exotic Places

Recreational Vehicle

Stop for a Hamburger

Attend a Festival

Go Electric

Visit a Park

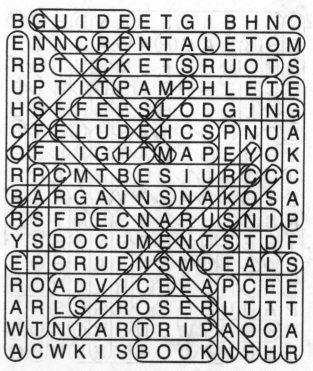

Travel Agent

Beverly Hills

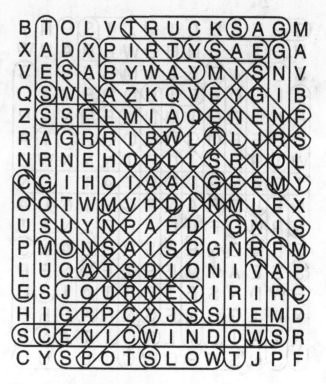

Sunday Drive

Vacation Destinations

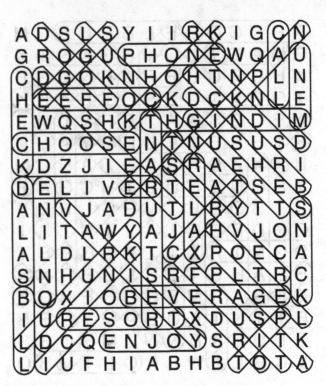

Ordering Room Service

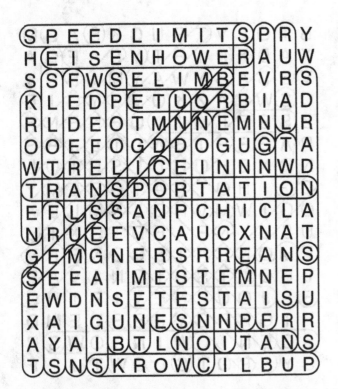

Interstate Highway System

Kentucky

Caribbean Vacation

Travel Expenses

Tour the Gardens

Traffic Report

Ski Vacation

Security Checkpoint

Houseguests

Vermont

Accommodations

Venice, Italy

Forest Explorer

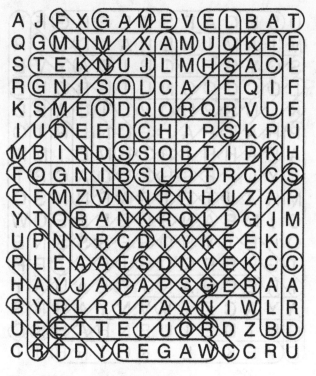

Casino Vacation

Around the World

```
N L A G U T R O P A I S A Y
G E T C A R O K G N A C Z L
R P G H I F A I D N I O I A
E O S E A R R L T R D T G T
E O R G J R I E I E J A L I
C U N L G M I M C M A O M M
E E O L I Z E W A A A A C N A
K N K Z N H D N N N H I D D A
U G G A T T A J Y D T E H A
W L N R I P N A N O C U P G
A A O B N Y A R I V R F O A
I N H X A G C O G E A R L S
T D N A L E R I E R T A E C
X Y E L O P H T R O N N O A
C H I N A E B B I R A C A R
G C O C I X E M A N T E I V
```

Travel Safety

```
D I M A C S T O U R U L E S
H E E D F U L I G H T S D D
P O L I C E N O I T U A C A
A S Y A W H G I H O T E L O
N L K T R Y S W I N D L E R
B S E S S N E C N E D U R P
U T U R G W S C S E R A C R
C E V I T N E T T A I K E E
K K S F O E N N T S V S L H
L C Y C N E G R E M E M U T
E I C O M A O C N A M O D A
C T H U B O U P R N B T E E
I P C R P R U C A P A S H W
V O I E I O H L A W S U C R
D A R T R E P O R T S C S L
A T Y G S F M O N E Y R A W
```

Miami

```
U S E C A P S N E E R G F F
M I A M I H E R A L D L L R
S O Y G F L O R I D A Y V E
L O C O C O N U T G R O V E
K L U S P U O V L I C A S D
P R A T P A L E C N L R I O
A E A H H I R T R M E I M M
L Y L P E S H K U O A C P T
M H J J T E I S W R N H S O
C I M R A N S D E E F E O W
O P E T Y R O S E S S S N E
T E E B P Q D R I P I T P R
T R E C N A N I F L A U A Y
A Y A C Z I V V N Y A R R S
G N I D L I U B N H A H K C
E Y E K L L E K C I R B J T
```

Auto Show

```
R O T O R S M O D E L I N E
Q N R R N M P I S T O N S K
O G U V O I M P O R T S Z A
B I C A T P E N G I N E V M
R S K N N A H C H R O M E S
U E S V K T L I G H T S H R
T D D E T A I L E D T S I A
Y I R Q I Z W Q T S T Y C C
R S B R A N D S U R N F L T
U P V I N T A G E E U A E P
X L U J H E X P E N S I V E
U Y C S I X X U M S O R D C
L R P H E E D I O L I E N
Y P O S T E K C I T C M B O
M E W M A E R D M O T S U C
P Y D K P O H S R E G A T S
```

Copenhagen

Safari

Travel Blogs

Weekend Getaways

Connecticut

Budget Travel

Visiting Relatives

Look at the Atlas

Drive a Car

Expensive Restaurants

Frequent Flyer

We Have EVERYTHING® on Anything!

The Everything® list spans a wide range of subjects, with more than 500 titles covering 25 different categories:

Business	History	Reference
Careers	Home Improvement	Religion
Children's Storybooks	Everything Kids	Self-Help
Computers	Languages	Sports & Fitness
Cooking	Music	Travel
Crafts and Hobbies	New Age	Wedding
Education/Schools	Parenting	Writing
Games and Puzzles	Personal Finance	
Health	Pets	

THE
EVERYTHING®
EASY LARGE-PRINT WORD SEARCH BOOK, VOLUME 2

Dear Reader,

Easy does it. That's my motto when it comes to puzzles. These word search puzzles are easy—that's what makes them so much fun. They will engage your brain without melting it down! With a gentle focus, words will appear in what seem like random letters. With enough concentration, even the last word will be revealed. You will return to the real world triumphant and refreshed.

It was a pleasure creating these puzzles for you. I've given each one a theme to make the solving more interesting. The grids have been loaded with relevant words. We used large print because bigger letters are better; finding the words is less tedious. Puzzles that are easy on the eyes are more fun for the brain.

So find a comfy chair and grab a pen or pencil. Get ready for a pleasant journey through these pages. Your brain will thank you for this relaxing diversion. Let's take it easy!

Charles Timmerman

Welcome to the EVERYTHING® Series!

These handy, accessible books give you all you need to tackle a difficult project, gain a new hobby, comprehend a fascinating topic, prepare for an exam, or even brush up on something you learned back in school but have since forgotten.

You can choose to read an Everything® book from cover to cover or just pick out the information you want from our four useful boxes: e-questions, e-facts, e-alerts, and e-ssentials. We give you everything you need to know on the subject, but throw in a lot of fun stuff along the way, too.

We now have more than 400 Everything® books in print, spanning such wide-ranging categories as weddings, pregnancy, cooking, music instruction, foreign language, crafts, pets, New Age, and so much more. When you're done reading them all, you can finally say you know Everything®!

PUBLISHER Karen Cooper

MANAGING EDITOR, EVERYTHING® SERIES Lisa Laing

COPY CHIEF Casey Ebert

ASSISTANT PRODUCTION EDITOR Melanie Cordova

ACQUISITIONS EDITOR Lisa Laing

EDITORIAL ASSISTANT Matthew Kane

EVERYTHING® SERIES COVER DESIGNER Erin Alexander

LAYOUT DESIGNERS Erin Dawson, Michelle Roy Kelly, Elisabeth Lariviere

Visit the entire Everything® series at *www.everything.com*

THE
EVERYTHING®
EASY
LARGE-PRINT
WORD SEARCH
BOOK
VOLUME 2

150 large-print easy word search puzzles

Charles Timmerman
Founder of Funster.com

Adams Media
New York London Toronto Sydney New Delhi

Adams Media
An Imprint of Simon & Schuster, Inc.
100 Technology Center Drive
Stoughton, MA 02072

An Everything® Series Book.
Everything® and everything.com® are registered trademarks of Simon & Schuster, Inc.

ADAMS MEDIA and colophon are trademarks of Simon and Schuster.

For information about special discounts for bulk purchases,
please contact Simon & Schuster Special Sales at 1-866-506-1949
or business@simonandschuster.com.

The Simon & Schuster Speakers Bureau can bring authors to your live event. For more information or to book an event contact the Simon & Schuster Speakers Bureau at 1-866-248-3049 or visit our website at www.simonspeakers.com.

Manufactured in the United States of America

17 2023

ISBN 978-1-4405-3889-6